DATE DUE

THE ART OF

Quarterbacking

by
KEN ANDERSON
with Jack Clary

Foreword by Paul E. Brown

Photographs by Jon Naso, Dennis Landwehr,
Mike Zagaris, Dilip Kane, John Monteleone,
Lou Witt, Chris and Donna Young

A Mountain  Lion Book

LINDEN PRESS/S&S
New York

Published by Linden Press/Simon & Schuster
A Division of Simon & Schuster, Inc.
Simon & Schuster Building
Rockefeller Center
1230 Avenue of the Americas
New York, New York 10020

LINDEN PRESS / SIMON & SCHUSTER
and colophon are trademarks of Simon & Schuster, Inc.

Designed by Irving Perkins and Associates
Manufactured in the United States of America

1   2   3   4   5   6   7   8   9   10

Library of Congress Cataloging in Publication Data

Anderson, Ken, date.
The art of quarterbacking.

"A Mountain Lion book."
Includes index.
1. Quarterback (Football) I. Clary, Jack T.
II. Title.
GV951.3.A6   1984   796.332′25   84-7193

ISBN 0-671-47651-3
0-671-50724-9 (Pbk)

ACKNOWLEDGMENTS

The authors would like to thank General Manager Paul Brown; Assistant General Manager Mike Brown; former Coaches Forrest Gregg and George Sefcik; Public Relations Director Allan Heim and his assistant, Ingrid Studley; equipment manager Tom Gray; trainer Marvin Pollins; players Turk Schonert, Dave Rimington, Mike Martin, Bobby Jackson, Rodney Tate, John Casanova, Steve Sullivan and Gary Cali; cinematographer Tom Sharkey; all of the Cincinnati Bengals; typists David Westlake and Rebecca S. Dunn; and for their help in setting up our demonstrations, Ed Croke and Tom Power of the New York Giants and Hal Lundgren of the San Francisco 49ers.

We would also like to thank Jon Naso of Mountain Lion Books for his superb stop-action photography, Mitch Cohen and Rick Spiller of Foto-Style, Dilip Kane and Bill Laznofsky for their photoediting, Buddy Skydell for his editing and direction, and John Monteleone of Mountain Lion Books for producing this book on schedule.

ACKNOWLEDGMENTS

Contents

Foreword

I always have believed that a quarterback, to be consistently successful, must possess two distinct sets of qualities. Of course, there are the physical attributes: he should have the proper size, speed and arm strength. But the nonphysical qualities are more important to the decision-making process whenever a team looks for a quarterback. First, I believe that a quarterback must be very intelligent. Secondly, he must be a sound person, stable, inwardly tough and determined to win.

Why?

A quarterback is the key man, a team's reflection, and you cannot build a sound organization on any level of competition if your leader does not have these personality traits.

Primarily, quarterbacks must earn their relationships with their fellow players by performing. The players must always feel they can win, because of their belief in what their quarterback can do. Years ago, when I coached the Cleveland Browns, the San Francisco 49ers had us down about thirty points in the first half and I was really exercised. Finally, a great running back we had on the team named Edgar (Special Delivery) Jones, came over to me and said, "Relax, coach, Otto will pull us out." The "Otto" was Otto Graham, now in the Hall of Fame, and he was a great quarterback. But even he couldn't do it for us on that day. Yet, thinking about that incident afterward, it occurred to me that Edgar Jones really believed in his quarterback.

Still, while the players must believe in their man, the quarterback must in turn be a performer, resolute under all conditions. That is why a determination to win and toughness within are two such important qualities a winning quarterback must possess. His teammates will sense, in very short order, whether or not he has them, and they will invest their belief in him accordingly.

Quarterbacks at every level also must be aware that much of their success is the end product of other people's efforts. Today, modern quarterbacks have tremendous help from their coaches in calling the plays. Occasionally, there is a quarterback who resents this, but most realize that it is done in the spirit of putting forth a total effort both by players and by coaches. The success of the team is the factor that counts.

Having played quarterback during my college football career at Miami University, in Oxford, Ohio, I know, for example, that a quarterback doesn't see very much downfield while he is handing off the ball to a running back, because his back is to the line of scrimmage. This means he does not always get a good look at how a defense reacts to his play. Therefore, he is really dependent upon those who do see what happens, for direction and guidance as the game progresses.

There also is no way that he can master all of the intricate detail in each week's game plan, because it is constantly changing. Today's game at most college and professional levels is computer football. A coach is always stationed in a spotting booth high above the field with the game plan, containing all the opposition's tendencies, which the computer has spat out. As the game progresses, he will observe just how precise these data are, and relay all up-to-date information to the coaches at field level. From this, the play is wigwagged or relayed to the quarterback.

This is the scientific way to call the plays and I have always believed that the real artistry of coaching is doing the right thing, the greatest possible number of times, under the stress of a game. In turn, the quarterback is the coach's man and he must carry this mental load on the field, even when the play is relayed to him. He must refine it as it comes from the sideline; he must add the starting count; he must be prepared to call a check-off for any defensive shifts he reads at the line of scrimmage which would imperil the play; and then lastly, but most importantly, he must perform.

Of course, when a quarterback is a prospect for a team there is no way any coach can ever be sure whether all of this will come to pass. In looking back over thirteen years, our selection of Ken Anderson, in the third round of the 1971 NFL draft, was the most fortunate selection we ever made, although at the time we drafted him, there were many unknown factors. Certainly, we knew that he possessed the physical capabilities to become an NFL quarterback. He was six feet three inches, weighed 212 pounds, and he could run. Bill Walsh, our wide receiver coach at that time, had worked him out and he liked his throwing motion and arm strength, as well as his overall athletic ability. My son, Mike, our assistant general manager, who had been a college quarterback at Dartmouth and knew the values we sought, also checked him out and he came back convinced that Ken could satisfy our need for a quarterback of the future.

In looking at the nonfootball side, we also found that Ken possessed those other qualities to which I referred earlier: he was very intelligent and he was a sound person. If there was a drawback, it was that he had played at the Division III level of competition in college. Taking him as high as the third round, we felt, was a real gamble.

Later, we found out in talking with the late Norm Van Brocklin, then the coach of the Atlanta Falcons, that he also was poised to select Ken on the same round. By good fortune, we drafted a few slots ahead of Atlanta that year. I subsequently have been told that Ken Anderson was a kind of open secret that many NFL teams hoped to keep to themselves, in order to draft him in later rounds.

Our taking him was a real gamble, but we never have regretted the choice, and he has been a credit to the game and to the Bengals.

In reflecting on Ken's career, the qualities that have made him so great are the same that made Otto Graham so great, and I was fortunate and privileged to have both on my teams during my coaching tenure in the NFL. They are qualities that any young man, wishing to perfect the quarterback position, should make every effort to emulate.

Paul E. Brown
Riverfront Stadium
Cincinnati, Ohio, 1984

Chapter 1
The Quarterback:
As a Player and a Person

WHAT is a quarterback?

Certainly, everyone knows that he is the player on a football team who directs the offense, whether it be by handing off the ball on a running play or passing it downfield to one of his backs or receivers. In a strict sense, he is the most important player on the team, because without him, nothing could happen. That is not meant to downgrade the importance of any other player, because in a team sport such as football, all the players must work together for everyone to succeed. Yet having defined what the quarterback is, and knowing the exact nature of football as a team sport, let me say that the quarterback also is the player who often gets too much credit when his team wins, just as he often gets too much blame when it loses.

The media and fans too often overlook the team aspects of football and the importance of every player doing his job on every play. The quarterback simply is the man who handles the ball and sees that it reaches the right player. If we did not have a great offensive line in Cincinnati, I could hand off the ball to one of our running backs and he wouldn't gain too much; or I could go back and try to pass to our great receivers, and before I could see who was open, the opposing defense would be sacking me.

Yet because we do have a great line, fine running backs and receivers, a great defense and kicking game, and a fundamentally sound system of plays, we are a successful football team. As a result, I have received a great deal of publicity, awards and notoriety, but I always have carefully pointed out in accepting these accolades that I do so only as one of forty-five players without whose combined efforts none of this would happen.

Before we get into the various elements that are important to becoming a good quarterback, I want to discuss what I consider some very basic principles that every quarterback should use as a suggested set of guidelines in his career. Most are concerned with the way he approaches the game, and how to handle the good and bad things that will eventually happen to him before he stops playing.

I've always maintained that there is much more to playing quarterback than having a strong arm, quick feet or great reflexes, though they all help. There have been many players with those attributes who have come into football, but because they lacked the right approach to how the game must be played and how they must conduct themselves, all of that talent has meant nothing.

It is always best to remember that while great quarterbacks can often make ordinary teams become better, great teams can make ordinary quarterbacks become stars. This is a principle that I never have lost sight of since coming to the Cincinnati Bengals as a third-round draft pick in 1971, probably because I came from a very small school, Augustana College, and really never had imagined achieving the success that has marked my career since then.

When I came to the Bengals, I didn't know how much was really involved in playing quarterback, with all of the intricacies and precise techniques that are so important to being successful. In reality, I started from scratch, and actually walked through the various physical maneuvers much as I have taught my own children to walk after they were able to stand. Even now, after so many years of playing, I still work to strengthen areas of my play that I feel need constant improving.

Of course, starting at such an elementary pace wasn't surprising, since I had played at a very small high school in my hometown of Batavia, Illinois, a town of about 11,000 some 60 miles southwest of Chicago, and then at Augustana where I was a roll-out quarterback who ran with the ball as often as I threw it. In high school, I was a defensive back as well as quarterback, but I obviously didn't play either position well enough to attract any major college scouts.

Actually, basketball was my sport, and I played on the same team as my neighbor and friend Dan Issel. Now Dan had the college basketball scouts pouring into town, and he finally went to the University of Kentucky, where he became an All-American player and later a great star in professional basketball.

I thought I played pretty well, too, and in deciding upon Augustana, it was with the primary intent of keeping my basketball career going. At the same time, I inquired whether I might find a job as a safety on the football team, pointing out that I had been an all-conference choice at that position in high school, and not pushing my quarterback qualifications too much.

When I came out as a college freshman, I was one of the biggest and fastest players on the squad, as big as some of the offensive linemen and faster than many of our other backs and the receivers. My coach for my final two years, Ben Newcomb, decided he'd take advantage of my speed and size, hence the emphasis on the roll-out type of offense. We were all successful with this system, something that really means more to me to this day than any kind of individual honors, and there were enough of those, including three years on the all-conference team, being named its outstanding player in my senior year, honorable mention Little All-American team, the MVP award from my teammates in my senior year, and being selected to play in the North-South All-Star Game.

Our passing game was good enough for me to be ranked among the NCAA College Division all-time leaders, and during my last two seasons, there were pro scouts from every team except my boyhood favorites, the Chicago Bears, watching me play. That is what I mean about a good quarterback making an ordinary team better, and a great team making a good quarterback a star. At Augustana, it was a bit of both, and in the end, I was the beneficiary.

But I've often thought that had I not played within the spirit of my team and not applied myself to the offense that Coach Newcomb had designed to take advantage of my particular talents, then all of the honors and rewards that have since happened with the Bengals never would have come to pass.

The message here is that despite your background—large or very small schools like mine—you can succeed if you apply all of your physical and mental talents while working wholeheartedly within the spirit of your team and your coaches. My first pro coach, Paul Brown, always told us that playing good football meant being in the spirit of the occasion, and his record of championships at every level of competition, his more than 300 victories and the legion of great players whom he helped to develop are ample proof that this point is valid.

And being in the spirit of your team also means being prepared to play at your best level and to set an example for all of the other players. Like it or not, the quarterback is the team leader, the man everyone looks to on the field—and off it as well—to get things done. As I said, he is often the player who gets too much of the credit for success. This sometimes can lead to problems among other players who might feel resentful that one player is getting so much credit. After all, a team is made up of different individuals, all with their own feelings, and if jealousy and resentment are allowed to build, then you can just about kiss goodbye any chances for success.

The best way to avoid these problems is to let the other players see you working just as hard as they do. This begins in the off-season when you work at the conditioning programs with your teammates. After all, as a member of the team you are expected to do everything in this area just as the most obscure player. Not only does it show good leadership, but it is important to build up your body so you can go all out from the first day of practice, and be able to avoid the injuries that could take you out of a game, and thus hurt your team's chances for success. (Later in the book, we'll discuss the various drills that I believe are important for a quarterback's development.)

If all of your teammates see you working as diligently as they do in the weight room, or if they see you out running and going through the same physical pain as they are, then there won't be any false notions that, as quarterback, you get special treatment or that you put yourself above the rest of the team. In training camp our former head coach, Forrest Gregg, used to put us through about six dozen grass drills—flopping on your stomach and leaping up again—before every practice session, and everyone who was not injured took part.

Anyone who has ever done these exercises—and Forrest learned them at Green Bay from his coach, Vince Lombardi—will admit they can be an almost insidious form of physical torture that punishes every body fiber. But quarterbacks are no different from rookies at this time, and we all do them. We did not like this—I suspect Forrest hated them at Green Bay, too—but you could imagine the reaction of the other players if he told the quarterbacks they were excused from the toughest part of our prepractice warm-ups.

That's just one part of being a team member—not putting yourself above everyone else. Another is to spread out the credit when you are successful and, going along with that, not pointing any fingers or criticizing other players when your team loses. There will be times when a back will fumble and lose the ball at a crucial time; or a receiver will drop one of your perfectly thrown passes, maybe for what could have been the winning touchdown; or one of your team's defensive backs will get beaten for a critical score. That is their problem and they feel even worse about it than you do. But there also may be games where your team loses because you have fumbled and lost the

17

ball, or thrown too many interceptions, or called the wrong plays, and they won't criticize you. Again, this comes down to football being a team game, where everyone wins as a team and loses as a team. In short, it means having respect for each other's efforts.

Many pro quarterbacks go out of their way to show their appreciation for the work that their teammates do. After our Super Bowl year in 1981, I bought our offensive linemen handsome briefcases, and I never have minded picking up a tab or two after practice when we sit around and relax. I also remember a story about a quarterback named Joe Kapp, who, after leading the Minnesota Vikings to the NFL conference title in 1969, became a member of the then Boston Patriots the following year. The first thing he did was to take his offensive linemen out to lunch, plunk a hundred-dollar bill on the bar and say, "Now, let's get to know each other very well."

Joe and the Patriots weren't very successful that year, but he certainly made an effort to let his linemen know in advance that he appreciated everything they could do for him. That was his style and he did it his way. That is important—do only what is your nature. In other words, don't be a phony. Team players, because they are thrown together to survive in all kinds of competitive situations, get to know each other very well, and they are the first to spot the player who is trying to be someone he really isn't. If a guy is really a gung-ho, go-get-'em type of player, then it will be natural for him to act that way. But if another guy is quiet, and suddenly tries to show the way by shouting and stomping about, it won't do a bit of good because his teammates will see right through the act.

Now this is not to say that when you might have to make a point with a word or two, don't do it. If you believe that's what it will take to get someone to pick up the pace a bit or pay attention, then you must do it. There are some individuals who need that kind of push, but if that's the case, do it within the framework of your own personality, the way in which you feel most comfortable.

Why is this necessary?

Remembering that you are the leader, if there are drastic changes in your personality your teammates will not be able to read you, to know just what you are trying to get across, and they won't know what to expect. Secondly, and just as important, they won't take you seriously because you are acting totally out of character. My teammates know that I'm not a shouter or screamer during a game or in practice. And the first time I did it in a game, they'd look at me as if I was crazy, and nothing good would come from that act. On the other hand, they know that if someone makes a glaring error, one look from me can show my displeasure. It is important that your fellow players know your personality and just how they can react to how you may feel. And a quarterback must be very careful to always give them that precise read on how he is feeling so that he can get the most from them.

This is particularly important during a game. The players always look to the quarterback for direction, and the one who maintains that even keel is the one who will be able to control the situation. I've never had a problem in this regard because of my own particular personality. My friend Dave Lapham, who was a starting offensive guard on the Bengals for more than half of my career, once said, "When things are going good, he's low-keyed. When things are going bad, he's low-keyed." I had to laugh at Cris Collinsworth during his rookie season when he said after a game that we won quite handily, "I thought Ken was going to fall asleep out there the way he was so low-keyed."

As I noted, that's just my personality, but it is important for every quarterback to keep that even keel. Remember Billy Kilmer, when he played quarterback for the Redskins? He was a fiery, vocal type of person who had a lot of emotional highs during a game, whether things went good or bad. Again, that was his even keel, and he was that way off the field, as well. It's important to keep in mind that a game can last a long time and that a lot of things are going to happen, good and bad, before it's over. So you've got to keep plugging all the time you're out there, and not get carried away with yourself. At the same time, you have to show some natural exuberance when something good happens. After all, you're part of the team, and it never hurts to let a player know he's done something extraordinary. In fact, this may be one of my weakest areas and something that I certainly concentrate on during a game.

Everyone has his own style. If Collinsworth made a great catch, I'd look at him and point a finger and he knew I appreciated that great play. It's the same with an offensive lineman who made a great block on a screen pass. You don't go hog wild but when everyone's in the huddle, you can say, "Hey, heckuva job out there, big boy." Now, he knows he made a good block, but to hear it from the quarterback in front of the other players just pumps him up and gives him a greater sense of pride about the good job that he has done. And you can bet that when he gets back to the line of scrimmage, he's going to blow that defensive guy right off his feet on the next play.

I'm as amazed as the fans when I see some astounding plays from our guys. I remember Isaac Curtis making a one-handed catch between two Steeler defensive backs on the sidelines that helped to win a game. I remember too many times when our receivers worked their butts off to break up an interception. A lot of people miss those things, but sometimes a receiver may work harder to keep the opposition from catching a bad throw than he does catching a good one from his quarterback. I still recall a game in Houston when I fumbled and one of the Oilers' linemen picked up the ball, which no one saw, and started running toward our goal line. Mike Wilson, one of our tackles, saw the guy and he chased him for sixty yards to stop the touchdown. You just know how much I appreciated that play.

Just to keep this in perspective, a quarterback doesn't have to go around backslapping and praising his players on every play. After all, they are expected to do their jobs but at special times—and there may be only four or five in an entire game—he certainly can flash the sign. Sometimes I've missed a great play, or didn't realize how really great it was, until I saw the films, and I've never been shy about yelling out my praise at that time to the particular player.

Now that's the good side. There also will be times in a game when things aren't going well. Maybe the quarterback has thrown a couple of interceptions or fumbled the ball, or the team is down by ten or twelve points. Just remember that game still is not lost, and the quarterback *cannot* go around with his head on his chest or grumbling about what a rotten day it is. He's got to keep the pressure on, to keep working so he can, hopefully, turn things around. One key in this regard—and we'll discuss more in greater detail later in the book—is to get back to basics. Go right to your most basic running play, give the offensive line a chance to regroup by coming off the ball and knocking someone down. Then go to pass patterns you feel the most comfortable with, so that everyone settles down a bit and gets back into a good rhythm. The record books are filled with stories of teams who've played horribly for a great deal of a game but still have come back to pull out a victory. We almost did it in Super Bowl XVI after trailing 20–0 at half time. Every one of us felt afterward that we really didn't lose; time just ran out to keep us from winning. That's because we never gave up.

One of the toughest times for me in recent years happened when I was taken out of our 1981 opening game against Seattle because I simply was not playing well. That will happen to every player who stays in this game long enough, but it didn't affect my personality or change the way I acted when we started to practice for our next game a few days later.

In fact, the guys started to kid me. "Tell us which side of the field you're going to throw the ball to so we can practice covering the interception," they would say. I just laughed and everyone knew it was part of the good-natured ribbing that everyone goes through.

The next Sunday, against the Jets in New York, the first play called from the sideline was a pass. When I stepped into the huddle, I said, "You won't believe this, but here comes a pass. Now everybody remember to cover." The guys all smiled and it really helped to relieve the tension. Oh, yes, the pass was complete and we went on to beat the Jets, 31–30.

All of this falls into the category of striving for respect, not popularity, though it certainly is possible to have both. So often young people have trouble separating the respect part from the popularity that they seek. The rule of thumb is simply that on a team that has anywhere from 45 to 95 players, depending on the level of competition, it is impossible to be popular or liked by everyone. There are too many diverse types of personalities, and they all have different likes and dislikes.

But it is possible to achieve everyone's respect in the way you work at your job. And that includes putting aside whatever personality conflicts that do occur and working for the same goal of team success. It is important that a quarterback, more than any other player, be meticulously careful, so personality conflicts don't become part of his daily life and allow his judgments to be colored.

That even means in his life outside the locker room. Every player on the team is not going to appeal to him as a friend or even acquaintance, so he should not strive to socialize with everyone just to show he can be popular. On our team, we have different groups who go out in social situations—married guys with married guys, the single guys with single guys, guys who'd rather entertain at home, guys who aren't very social and like quiet times. That's fine because the interests of each group are compatible. But when we get to practice, those things are left behind and we work with just one interest—the Cincinnati Bengals.

I've always enjoyed the four weeks at training camp because it is a period of time when I can leave some of my family responsibilities behind and go out with my teammates. It gives me a chance to go out after practice when everyone's dog-tired, have a beer and complain with everyone else about the coaches and the way things have gone. For me, it is a necessary time of togetherness, but it doesn't alter my approach to our preparation when we hit the practice field the next morning.

All of this is tied up in being the team's nominal leader, and I want to make the distinction here between the quarterback as leader and the team's captains as its leaders. Often, nonquarterbacks are chosen to be captain because they have extraordinary leadership ability, and the players look up to them for guidance and as someone they can go to for a quiet discussion about a problem concerning the team, the coach or about their status on the club. Many coaches do not want their quarterback to be a captain because of the unique relationship the player must maintain with him, the mental burdens of preparing for a game, and then the responsibilities that are his in directing the team during a game.

The team captain is the team's overall leader, and even during a game, he can set the example or rally his fellow players to play harder. But the quarterback is the player to whom everyone, including the captain, directs his attention during the game. The quarterback runs the show on the field, but he and the captains must work together and must respect each other's roles for the benefit of the team. When I joined the Bengals, Bob Johnson, our center who retired after the 1980 season, was the offensive captain and we became great friends. I always respected his role as captain just as I did that of his successor, Archie Griffin, one of our running backs, and that of Jim Le-Clair, a linebacker who was the defensive co-captain.

These leadership roles are not the result of popularity contests but are the product of being respected by one's teammates. Again, I must stress the importance, particularly for young players, of not worrying about being popular, though I'll be the first to admit that anybody who is an athlete really wants to be popular with the fans. This is different from seeking popularity with your teammates, because every athlete wants to do well in front of those who come out to watch him play and to hear the cheers that will result.

Let me assure you there is nothing better than listening to a stadium filled with fans cheering your efforts; and there is no greater feeling than walking back into your locker room after a game as part of the winning team. There is a tangible bond that exists between every player on the team, knowing that they played well together and were successful. Of course, there also are times when the team wins and they didn't play well, and everyone will know that, too. And if players get too carried away under these conditions, our coaches always have been the first to tell us that, "Yes, you won, but you didn't play well doing it, and you will have to play better next week." And they back that up with some tough film critiques and practice sessions the following week.

But the key here is that no one, especially quarterbacks, should get so carried away that he becomes obsessed with winning in everything he does. I'm not talking about a football game; that is a necessary obsession and it requires a player's total mental and physical energies tightly focused on one opponent.

Yet away from the field, every player—every person—should keep a perspective on winning. I love to play golf and tennis and I certainly like to win when I play, but having a good time and relaxing under those conditions is more important for me than the ultimate winning or losing of the match.

I know that Coach Lombardi often has been quoted as saying, "Winning isn't everything, it's the only thing," and many people have criticized him for taking what they consider a win-at-all-costs approach. What he really said, and what has been sometimes conveniently dropped by those wishing to make winning in athletics a sort of personal scapegoat, was, "Winning isn't everything, *but making the effort to win* is the most important thing."

By this, he of course meant that if a player or a competitor gives every game his best effort, he will be successful more times than not. He also will not cheat himself or his teammates, and he will realize the values that come from that all-out effort, something that the person can carry away from the athletic field and use in every phase of life.

Every player, quarterback or not, must remember that you can't win every game. You try to because that's the ultimate goal, and the more you win, the more successful you and your team will be. But as I noted before, you must keep winning in perspective—a win when you played well is most satisfying; a win when you didn't is a win, but there isn't the same satisfaction for me. Coach Brown used to tell us when we won a tough game to walk out with our heads high, and if we lost a game where we also played well to do the same thing because we had nothing to be ashamed of.

There have been many times when we have won by three or four touchdowns but I've come away disappointed because I didn't play as well as I thought I could. By the same token, there have been times when I prepared myself thoroughly during the week and played as well as I could during the game and we lost. I hated to lose, and all the work and effort don't necessarily diminish the pain of losing, but I could walk away with my self-respect, knowing that I did everything possible. It was just one of those days that didn't work out. I can live with myself better under those circumstances than I can when, after we won, I knew that I cheated myself during the week by perhaps socializing a bit too much or didn't put forth the same mental preparation.

I'm not the only player to experience those feelings; there are plenty of guys on my own team and elsewhere in the sport who take great pride in the job that they do and how it will affect their team. It is part of their attitude and desire to be a part of a winning situation.

If you are the quarterback, one of the realisms that very quickly hits you in the face is that it's not going to be all cheers. There'll be boos when things aren't going well. You'll be called a great leader when your team is winning, and a lousy leader when it isn't, though you still are the same person trying to do the same things. I don't know of any quarterback who hasn't experienced this kind of roller-coaster existence at one time or another, and that includes those who are in the Hall of Fame.

If you play college and professional football, the mail will come during your bad times telling you to hang it up and blaming you for all of the team's problems. Part of the problem is that the fans sit up in the stands, look down and see tiny little guys running around a football field. They don't think of you as being people such as they are, and that like them, you too will have ups and downs in your career. The moment of truth always comes in situations where you meet fans face-to-face; but even in our bleakest seasons, I never had any bad experiences, though some of those same people might have booed me the previous Sunday. As I said before, the quarterback gets too much credit for winning and too much blame for losing.

Quarterbacks must have thick hides. A few years ago I was injured in a game, and as I lay on the Riverfront Stadium turf while the doctor worked on me, I could hear people cheering . . . cheering because I was injured and would have to come out of the game. I later referred to the ones who did that as "jerks," and I never had any reason to regret what I said. Regardless of the level of competition, there is no reason to cheer because a player is injured. The fans who do such a thing would run like scared rabbits if the player confronted them or, maybe worse, would play the hail-fellow, well-met, and pretend to be one of their great fans.

Nobody likes to be booed. Everybody wants to be popular to the extent of hoping the fans will think he is doing a good job, and when the booing begins, it hurts inside. You try to block it out of your mind, and it happened to me enough at the midpoint of my career, when our team had three consecutive losing seasons, that I learned to ignore it pretty well.

But all young quarterbacks will learn quickly enough that there are a lot of ups and down with the fans. I found it hard to understand during our down time because I had such good years early in my career, with two play-offs and a string of winning seasons, that it really came as a bit of a shock that the fans would forget about that and blame me for losing seasons. But fans don't understand that players are their own worst critics, and when they are not playing well, they usually are harder on themselves than any fans ever could be.

But recognition, good and bad, comes with the quarterback's territory. You never like criticism but you get used to it and you learn to accept that which is justified. The key is keeping your cool. Don't yell at the fans, don't make obscene gestures and, as I mentioned before, don't blame your teammates, even though their play might be directly affecting your own. This is simply part of the mental discipline that a quarterback must have in order to be successful at his job. The ones who can survive these low moments and not let them affect their performance will eventually become successful; those who don't will just fall by the wayside. It's happened so often in pro football where great college quarterbacks are drafted by poor teams, and before the team can build some strength, the quarterbacks have some terrible games or even some terrible seasons and simply become what I call "gun-shy." All of the negative experiences, on and off the field, have dulled their skills to such an extent that they simply cannot perform to the level that once was predicted for them.

At the same time, a quarterback who isn't playing well must expect to be criticized, and he must find a way to get himself back to a level of excellence. When you perform in the public eye, you have to expect to be scrutinized and judged. When I was lifted in that Seattle game, I wasn't playing well, and I hadn't played well in the preseason games, either. So it was Coach Gregg's prerogative to take me out of that game, which we later won; and he also displayed enough faith in my ability to recover from the experience that he put me right back in as the starting quarterback the following week against the Jets.

When a quarterback has those negative experiences, he can't give up on himself, whether he be a ten-year veteran, as I was, or someone just starting out. He must continue to prepare as if he were on top of the world and work as hard at the game as if he were competing with a legion of all-stars. We'll discuss the preparation phase of the quarterback's job later in the book, but for now it's enough to say that in the pros he gets paid as much for practicing as he does for playing, and he is expected to work just as hard at it as he does in a game.

Professional players have an opportunity to continue their football study on a year-round basis. I often spend three days a week with our offensive coaches during the off-season looking at film, discussing the merits and demerits of our passing game, and working with them to try and come up with a more effective offense for the coming season. I do this in addition to working out and throwing the ball when the weather permits and in general keeping my own game tuned up.

In other levels of football, quarterbacks also can work with their coaches as time and class schedules permit, and they certainly should maintain a consistent mental and physical fitness program during the off-season. The important thing to remember from all of this is that though he is often the essential ingredient in a team's success, the quarterback still must prepare as diligently and painstakingly as every other player. He is charged with leading the team by example and being, at all times, the guiding force no matter how tough the situation. We shall see just how much is involved in this responsibility as the quarterback's role unfolds in succeeding chapters.

Chapter 2
The Mechanics of Ball Handling

QUARTERBACKING is no different from any of the other so-called glamour occupations because there are certain duties that must be performed before all of the spectacular things begin to unfold. I've always equated the process with moviemaking. Actors will rehearse a scene many times and then may have to repeat it in front of the camera a dozen more before the director is satisfied. When I see the movie, that scene is just one part of an excellent entertainment package.

Well, before the quarterback can begin doing his job, everything starts in the same unspectacular manner, with all of the players gathered in the huddle to hear the play, a very important first step that ultimately leads to the kind of offensive formation to be used, a correct reading of the defense, proper checking of all assignments for the play and the final execution of the run or pass, with all of the intricacies that will help make it successful.

The huddle, as we know it, with all eleven players gathered together, was popularized just over sixty years ago to combat crowd noise, though Amos Alonzo Stagg had used one when his University of Chicago teams played indoors at the Chicago Coliseum around the turn of the century. But it wasn't until Bob Zuppke, one of football's greatest innovators, became head coach at the University of Illinois in the early twenties that the use of the huddle became widespread. Until then signals were shouted at the line of scrimmage and the play was off and running. The defense often would try to disrupt this procedure by shouting and making noise, so Zuppke decided to gather his players in a group about five yards from the ball. At first, this was seen as unsportsmanlike and the rules committee at that time threatened to have it outlawed. But no action was ever taken and the idea of players huddling caught on in the surge of popularity that followed Zuppke's teams featuring the immortal Red Grange.

The most common are the round and oval huddles. The latter may be formed east and west (in the same direction as the line of scrimmage), or north and south (pointing up and down the field). In the fifties, Frank Leahy, the coach at Notre Dame, came up with a "talking" huddle, in which everyone stood facing the quarterback, who then talked directly to each player in giving the play.

The type to be used really is a coach's preference, and if there is any real edge, I think the east-west huddle is the best because the quarterback's voice is contained in a very small area with the other players acting as a barrier to help keep out crowd noise.

The successful use of the huddle is up to the quarterback. His voice must be heard, and it must be clear and carry to all the other ten players. He must keep his head up, face the players across from him, and speak very clearly and with confidence and authority. If he doesn't believe in the play, how is the rest of the offense going to believe in it? Don't allow words to run together. For example, I may call, "This is from up on two," repeating it twice, and then say, "Split right, 90 double quick out from up on two."

That is quite a mouthful but everyone has to hear every word and understand exactly what I have just said. It is not uncommon for numbers or words to run together, and that is why players often botch up their assignments. At the same time, the quarterback must speak loudly enough to be heard only in his own huddle. The defense is standing just ten yards away, and there always are a couple of sharpies who try to pick up the snap count or some of the terminology that will tip them as to whether the play will be a run or a pass.

Outdoors, crowd noise can help keep you from being overheard by the defense, but oddly enough, we have found that in an indoor stadium, such as the Astrodome, if there are not many people or if the crowd is unusually quiet, a quarterback's voice can carry farther than he thinks. Conversely, if the crowd is roaring, he may also have to increase his own volume to be sure his voice is heard in the huddle because that noise bounces off the roof and back down to the playing field.

We work on calling plays in the huddle from the first day of training camp, and we do so in each day's double practice sessions. The first comes shortly after our warm-ups when the offense is broken down to units of eleven, and each unit works on timing and getting off on the snap count as one man. The quarterback will form a huddle, call a play and then rapidly have his unit execute it. While the intent of this drill is to polish unit execution, it also drills each player into the discipline that must be part of the huddle. Later in each practice when we are working on specific plays, we'll also begin each play from the huddle, even though every player knows beforehand what the play will be. Again, it is part of grooving an offensive unit in every facet of the discipline that will be part of its execution during a game.

By the discipline of a huddle, I mean that it is not the place for debating. Once we form up, the quarterback is the only player who will talk. If one of our guys wants to tell me something, he has to get to me while we are forming up and before I turn to the sidelines to see which play is being signaled in, or after we return to the bench following an offensive series.

Now if there is a question after the play is called, a player will say, "Check." That tells me to repeat the play. Sometimes a player will draw a blank and not remember his assignment, and it is the quarterback's job to tell him. That means the quarterback should know all of the assignments for each play, which, after a number of years, shouldn't be too difficult because of his familiarity with the team's offensive system.

This really has helped me because there are certain blocking moves a center must make which cause some difficulty in taking the snap. Sometimes he's got to pull out or move at a particularly difficult angle to make his block, and if I'm aware of what these particular moves are, then I can adjust myself a little bit to make sure that I get the snap. It may mean staying there just a fraction of a second longer to be sure I have the ball while he goes into his blocking maneuver.

I recall a play we used when Bob Johnson was the Bengals' center that gave the two of us so much trouble we actually were missing snaps. It turned out the problem came from one particular move that he had to make. It tuned me in to paying closer attention to the line calls, which are checks on blocking assignments a center will call out when he reaches the line of scrimmage. When I heard that particular move being called, I would ride him just a little bit more to be sure that I got the ball.

While the center is making the line calls, the quarterback also should be checking the defensive alignment. There will be a couple of times every season when the defense will not cover one of the wide receivers, and all the quarterback wants to do then is to get the ball and throw it to him. I remember a game against the Steelers when one of our backup quarterbacks broke the huddle and went to the line of scrimmage at Pittsburgh's five-yard line. He looked from right to left as if he was checking everything, except that he missed seeing Isaac Curtis lined up with no defensive coverage. Isaac was waving at him and hollering for the ball, but the quarterback never saw him. If he had, all he had to do was throw the pass and Ike could have strolled into the end zone for a touchdown. Instead, we had to settle for a field goal.

The lesson here, of course, is to really see something when you start looking right and left. Often you can pick up the pre-snap alignment in the defensive coverage. You might notice that one of the linebackers or defensive backs is cheating up a bit, or edging upward on his toes, which could indicate he'll be blitzing or going into a certain type of coverage. See everything and you'll cut down your mistakes—and make some very big plays.

A note of caution here: Many quarterbacks, knowing where the play is going, have a tendency to check that area with more attention than the rest of the defense. That's a bad habit and it can tip off the defense to where the play will go. It happened to me in college; an official told me after one of our games, "I could tell exactly which side of the field you were going to run the ball to."

"How could you do that?" I asked him.

"If you were going to run to the right side, you would look to the left and then look to the right just before the ball was snapped. If you were going to the left, you would look to the right, and then to the left just before you took the ball," he replied.

The key here is to make sure not to follow the same pattern all the time so the defense can foretell your actions.

However, a quarterback still must take some care to check the area where the play is going so he won't run into an overshifted defense. If he sees that happening and his offensive system has a series of audibles or alternate plays, then he can change the play at the line of scrimmage. He also should look for such things as a cornerback playing extremely loose, or well back from the line of scrimmage. Here, he also might want to check off or change the play, and throw a quick "out" or a "hitch" pass for five or six yards. Another good reason for scanning the defense is that while the quarterback may not be able to read the precise defensive coverages, he might be able to eliminate two or three possibilities. It makes his job after the snap a lot easier.

The quarterback also must check his own alignment, being sure that his

29

backs are in the right position if there is to be a running play, and pay particular care that he has a legal formation—that is, that there are at least seven men on the line of scrimmage, a receiver at each end of the line, and that the players are at least one yard behind it.

I remember one game when I went up to the line of scrimmage, looked down the line and thought I saw one of our linemen already lined up offside. I went to tell him that he was beyond the ball only to discover that I had taken a position behind a guard and was actually looking at our center, who by the rules is allowed to extend his body farther than the other linemen, though not beyond the peak of the ball. Had I not noticed this, I would have been hunkered down behind the guard awaiting a snap of the ball that never would have come. So if nothing else, that little move saved me tons of embarrassment.

This is a particularly important time for every offensive player, and it is one that demands the quarterback's total attention. First, he has only a stipulated number of seconds to run the play. The offensive linemen are busy checking their assignments and honing in on their line calls, so he must allow them enough time to be ready and try not to run the play beforehand. He must check the alignment of his backs to see that they are in the proper position for the play, though with the increased use of a single setback, he'll normally be right behind the quarterback. And if backs and receivers shift prior to the snap of the ball, he must be sure that everyone finally is in place and set for at least one second before the play begins, as stipulated by the rules.

During all of this, the defense is allowed to make as many shifts as it wishes, and in so doing it may force the quarterback to call an audible. A key to coping with an always shifting defense is to get to the line of scrimmage and go on quick counts—after the team is set for that one second—so the defense doesn't have time to continue its shifts. If a defense gets caught off-balance a couple of times, it will settle down a bit, often to the quarterback's advantage.

The Dallas Cowboys are famous for all of their shifting on offense, punctuated by the offensive line standing up prior to the play beginning. That is simply designed to mask, for a moment, the final formation. This can confuse the defense by making the players change their individual defensive keys every time an offensive formation is changed. Jack Lambert, the great middle linebacker of the Steelers, told me that when he played against Dallas for the first time in Super Bowl X, he was often at least one formation shift behind in recognizing his defensive responsibilities. Other teams have copied this, but the end result is that when all of the shifting and movement are finished, the Cowboys and their clones will finally operate from familiar formations. Tom Landry, prior to becoming head coach at Dallas, had been a great defensive innovator with the New York Giants, and he knew that the theory of successful defense depended on each player picking up the keys, or clues, that the offense would offer from its alignment. Destroy those keys, he reasoned, or at least confuse the defensive players long enough with so many formation changes, and an offense has a better chance to succeed.

When the offense finally is set, the quarterback must get it going with his voice. The key is to be sure that it can be heard from one side of the field to the other, particularly if he changes the play at the line of scrimmage. Often, he'll have a flanker 20 or 25 yards away or a receiver going in motion away from him, so his voice must carry at least that far, and above all of the normal crowd noise. We'll discuss what to do in extraordinary noise situations later in this chapter.

There are two kinds of snap counts—rhythmic and nonrhythmic. Obviously, the *rhythmic snap count* is always the same tempo: "Hut one . . . hut two . . . hut three," with the same pause between each sound. Or it can be just "hut," or "go," or whatever signal is being used to get a team off the ball. The benefit of this tempo is that it helps a team get moving quicker with less chance of error, and this is particularly important for a young team or for young quarterbacks who are trying to establish a cadence. This kind of cadence or tempo also is important in having all of a team's quarterbacks calling signals the same way; it is helpful for the backs and linemen when they must work with a new quarterback during the game.

The problem with a constant use of the rhythmic count is that the defense can also pick up the tempo, and that gives it an edge. The answer to this is the *nonrhythmic cadence*, where there can be a short pause—or a pause as long as you want—between the "huts." It would sound like this: "Hut . . . hut-hut . . . hut . . . hut-hut-hut." This system particularly helps the offensive linemen because they know when the ball will be snapped and can get the first jump on the defense which now cannot anticipate any particular rhythm.

We go right back into the huddle to help make this successful, because the quarterback must alert his players that he will be doing something different, if he doesn't use the nonrhythmic cadence all the time. Remember, the other players get used to the way that he calls out his signals and he must tell them that it will be different on this play so they won't move before the ball is snapped or go offside and cause their team to be penalized.

He can say, "All right, listen up, guys. We're going to try to pull them offsides. We're going to go on a three count, but it's going to be nonrhythmic." They know that no matter how quickly—or how long—it takes to call out that third signal, they cannot move until they hear it. If the defense is used to a team going on two or three rhythmic counts, it might move on what it anticipates as being the snap count.

There are a couple of other little tricks a quarterback can use to his advantage when calling signals. The first is with his *voice inflection*. I've been able to combine the nonrhythmic with a change in my voice pitch. This works well when our players know that if I'm going to go on the third sound, they may hear a little voice inflection on the second one; if it's a four count, they may get it on the first and then again on the third count.

One of the advantages is that if a quarterback tends to go on the second "hut" a lot, then he suddenly makes the snap count on three but increases his voice on that second count, he might get a defensive guy to react to that rising voice inflection and jump offside. I like to use this in situations where I want to throw the ball across the middle into a tight spot, and try to get an easier five yards from the penalty. If it happens, I get a free play and I then have a better chance of using a higher percentage play to get my first down. If it's third-and-four and the change in pitch gets a defensive lineman to jump, I get a free first down.

Several years ago, I used voice inflection to help us get a tough 10–7 vic-

31

tory over the Browns, when Cleveland jumped offsides ten times during the game. Three of those came in the first quarter when we were en route to scoring our only touchdown. On another occasion against Oakland, it helped to nullify two interceptions by the Raiders' defense, and both times I caught a defensive end named Willie Jones. I should have gotten him on a third try but the officials didn't call it and he leveled me to such an extent I had to leave the game for a couple of plays.

However, be judicious in using it because, obviously, the more it's done the less effective it will be. Also, don't use it so that it will backfire and cause your guys to move and get a five-yard penalty.

A quarterback can also use the nonrhythmic count, voice inflection and then add the *head bob.* Moving your head up and down in rhythmic fashion is very natural when forcefully calling signals, and officials will not bother you as long as the motion goes one way all of the time. But they will call a penalty if you jerk it with the obvious intent of drawing the defense offside. The key is to combine the rising voice inflection with a slightly accentuated head movement. Bob Griese, when he played with the Dolphins, was a master of this technique, and I've found it has some advantages, though I get called about once a season by the officials. But a note of caution: This is something that only experienced quarterbacks should try to use, and only after they have perfected the nonrhythmic snap cadences.

I've often been asked what happens if a player forgets the snap count after he leaves the huddle. That happens all the time but the running backs and linemen aren't the only ones who suffer those lapses. So do the quarterbacks—me specifically, early in my career at Augustana. Our center turned around and said, "What's the snap count?"

I couldn't remember but I was too embarrassed to admit it, so I said, "Well, if you don't know, I'm not telling you."

Of course, we went offside on the play, and I was dead wrong for not calling time-out or just making something up.

Bengals linemen often play games with the snap count, too. Our center may ask the guard at the line of scrimmage, "What's the snap count?"

"On two?" the guard might say, and if Mean Joe Greene was across the line of scrimmage, he'd hear it and pass it on; and pretty soon, just about everyone in the stadium would know the ball was to be snapped on the second sound. Of course, they were trying to foul up the defense, since both of them knew that wasn't the count at all, but they often had me confused because sometimes I believed them. I always figured those were some of the little games that linemen like to play with the quarterback just to keep him honest.

But if a player does not hear the snap count in the huddle or can't understand it, he should, as noted earlier, say, "Check," or whatever code word the team uses for such instances. There's also nothing clearer than saying, "I didn't catch the count," or "Tell me again." We've had instances where a guard or tackle might forget while walking to the line of scrimmage, and he'd hold two fingers behind his back. If that was the number, I'd say, "Right." If not, he'd try three or one, or whatever, until getting it right. And it worse really comes to worse, every offensive player can watch the ball out of the corner of an eye, and when it moves, he can move. This is particularly true for wide receivers, who often have a tendency to take off when they see a defensive lineman move. That should never happen because that lineman may be jumping prematurely, and if our guy goes before the ball is snapped and the defensive lineman gets back without making contact with an offensive player, then the offense gets tagged with a five-yard penalty. Even if the defensive guy gets flagged, so does the receiver, and we lose an easy five-yard penalty because of the offsetting violation.

Wide receivers also are victims of crowd noise in trying to catch the snap cadence or a play change when the quarterback hollers out the words or numbers that signal the change. A quarterback must yell out the change twice, looking first to the left, and then repeating it again looking to the right. Wide receivers generally will be looking in toward the line of scrimmage before a play begins so they can better hear the snap count, so you will have their attention when you direct your voice toward them.

Dealing with crowd noise—and this is a problem found more at the major college and professional level—requires some attention. None of us will forget Super Bowl XVI when we had a second down and a yard to go at the San Francisco 49ers' one-yard line. I called Pete Johnson on an off-tackle run to the left. The play also brought a flanker in motion to that side of the field so that he could block the outside linebacker. When I began to call signals, that linebacker moved right into the spot where Johnson was to go. So with a voice signal I changed the flanker's route as he came in motion, directing him to help lead the play and blow out the linebacker. But the crowd noise was so intense in the Silverdome that he never caught the audible and maintained his original course. Of course, the linebacker stayed there untouched and helped to stack up the play for no gain, as part of that heartbreaking series of plays that left us without any points.

Crowd noise is one of the distractions that a quarterback must endure, and we'll discuss more about that later in this book. But in calling signals, he must take some caution as to how he copes with the situation. The key is to be cognizant of the rules, most of which are standard at every level of play.

Crowd noise usually builds even before the quarterback reaches the line of scrimmage, and he should be able to judge right then whether or not his team can hear the signals. If he decides it cannot, rather than risk a bad play the quarterback can (1) hold both of his hands above his head, asking for quiet, or (2) ask the referee to signal for an official, or referee's, time-out if the crowd does not respond immediately. This, in effect, asks for the official's opinion as to whether the noise is too great for the linemen to hear the signals. The referee, if he agrees, then will stop the clock (both the game clock and the special 25- or 30-second clock) until such time as he feels the quarterback should begin his signal calling. Then, there are times when the noise will reach overwhelming crescendos after the quarterback has begun calling signals. If that happens, he should not raise up or lift his hands from under the center because the defense might react to that move and he will get called for a movement penalty. I always keep my hands in place and ask the umpire, who is standing in front of me behind the defensive line, for an official's time-out because my linemen can't hear. And I don't move until I see him make the time-out signal.

During these instances, the quarterback has to remember that when the official signals to resume play, the 25- or 30-second clock also will not resume from the point where it stopped. In college and high school football, the game clock also will start at that time; in pro football, it restarts when the ball is snapped.

Roger Staubach once was involved in an Army-Navy game where this situation proved to be the final edge in his Navy team coming away with a victory. Army, trailing by six points, had the ball at the Middies' goal line with less than a minute to play. The crowd noise was so great in Philadelphia's John F. Kennedy Stadium that the Army quarterback, Rollie Stichweh, asked the referee to quiet the crowd. He signaled for a time-out, stopping the clock so the noise would diminish. Seeing this, the Army team moved back to its huddle. Stichweh thought the clock would not resume until the ball was snapped. Unfortunately, this was not true, and he didn't see the referee's signal to restart the clock. Precious seconds started to tick away while he had his team in the huddle, and when he heard the crowd screaming at him, he finally realized—too late—that time was running out. Army never did get off another play and just missed pulling off a momentous upset.

All of the things we have discussed thus far in this chapter have brought us to the point where the quarterback is ready to take the ball from his center. Much that a quarterback will do here depends on the physical makeup of that center. A short center will not bring the ball up as far as a taller center, so you must put your hand farther under him. If he is tall, you don't have to bend your knees as far, and you'll be in a more upright position. With the Bengals, both Bob Johnson and Blair Bush were fairly tall, so I always stood up pretty straight and had my hands positioned farther back, never feeling that I'd get tied up with their blocking maneuvers. On the other hand, Dave Rimington, our newest center, is shorter, and I have to bend down a bit more to get the ball.

It is important that a quarterback be comfortable when he sets himself to take the ball. He should set his feet so that he can move any way he wishes without getting tangled up or being off balance. I try to have mine about shoulder width apart, with the weight evenly distributed, though sometimes I "mentally" put the weight on the foot that I will use to push away from the center.

Quarterbacks also can set their feet to take a predetermined cheat step, something that was frowned upon when I came into pro football. A good example of a cheat step comes from a story that Paul Brown enjoys telling about the first game his old Cleveland Browns team ever played, which was against the Miami Seahawks of the old All-America Football Conference, and that team had a quarterback who planted his feet deeply under the center and all but squatted down to take the snap. He'd have to uncork and take deliberate backward steps to get away, and in that game Coach Brown still marvels at the job that his middle guard, Bill Willis, did in knifing across the line of scrimmage and sacking that poor guy time after time.

"We let Otto Graham, our quarterback, have one foot slightly behind the other so he could get out quicker," Coach Brown added. "We had to because Willis, who also played offensive guard, was so quick in stepping to make his block he'd often crunch Otto's toes."

I know what Otto went through because Max Montoya, one of our guards, did the same to me during a game against Houston a couple of years ago, so we went to the practice field and worked out the problem. A little cheat step is not a bad idea because it does help the quarterback get away from the center quicker and not get tangled up in any of the guards' blocking maneuvers. At the same time, he must not plant his feet so the defense will know what he's going to do on the play.

Coach Brown often told the story of how Alex Agase, one of his old Cleveland linebackers, was so adept at picking up these little tips that he was able to outfox the Philadelphia Eagles when the two teams—both champions of their respective leagues—met for the first time in 1950. Agase had noted from film study that Eagles quarterback Tommy Thompson stood one way when he was going to hand off the ball, and then another when he planned to pass. During the game, he simply signaled his defensive mates whether the play would be a run or pass and this went a long way in helping the Browns win, 35–10.

Hand placement to receive the ball depends on the center and the type of snap that he makes. Our centers give the ball about a quarter turn, so I set my right hand on the natural curvature of their butt, and the left hand is below it, palm up, forming a V. Sometimes if the center snaps the ball straight back without rotating it, the quarterback may have both hands on the center's butt and take the snap in that manner.

I never worry too much about how far the fingers are spread because the ball comes up endwise and it's easy to grab. I place my hands so that my thumbs are together, and by sliding my left thumb downward a bit, I form a natural groove for the ball. At the same time, I keep enough pressure on the center's butt with my upper hand so that he'll know where I want the ball to land. When he snaps it, the ball will hit something solid—my hand—and he'll immediately release it. At the same moment the bottom hand comes up and secures it.

The hand position is important. If a quarterback doesn't get the ball with his top hand, or if it hits the bottom hand first, he can't secure it, and that is when fumbled snaps occur. Keeping pressure on the center's butt not only gives him a target for placing the ball, but prevents him from splitting the quarterback's hands. Some centers are so strong that they really don't realize the force of their snaps. Being unaware of this, or not giving them a spot to aim for, is when the ball can split hands and wind up either in a quarterback's stomach or on the ground.

Once the quarterback has taken the snap, he should immediately draw the ball back onto the plane of his stomach and secure it there with both hands before he either hands it off or raises it into the passing position. Don't move too far with the ball extended because pulling guards, flailing elbows and people getting pushed backward can knock it loose. Young or inexperienced quarterbacks, particularly, seem so concerned about making the handoff that they often forget to protect the ball. Later in the book, we'll discuss some drills that will help young QBs master this technique.

Before we discuss the types of handoffs, it is best to point out that centers and quarterbacks should work together as much as possible to polish their techniques of snapping and accepting the ball. This is particularly important for a pass play, where the ball should come into the quarterback's hands with

35

2-1

2-2

2-3

2-4

2-5

To take the snap, my feet are shoulder width apart and
my weight is evenly distributed (photo 2-1). My right hand
measures a comfortable distance (photo 2-2), my knees
are flexed and my right hand is firmly against the center's
butt (photos 2-3, 2-4). My thumbs are together, with the
left one downward a bit (photos 2-5, 2-6). The snap will
hit my top hand first and then be secured by the bottom
hand (photo 2-7).

2-6

2-7

37

2-8

the laces ready to grasp for the proper throwing position. Centers can set the ball for that precise kind of snap as soon as they reach the line of scrimmage.

In handing off the ball, the most important thing the quarterback should remember is that he must "see" the ball into the running back's hands. A back may form a pocket with his hands together or his arms apart to receive the ball, but the burden is on the quarterback to place the ball in that area, and he must do so with his eyes as well as with his hands—not just make a stab at where he thinks the spot will be.

If the quarterback is on the back's left side as he heads for the line of scrimmage, then the runner's left elbow will be in the air and his right arm will be underneath, forming the pocket in which the quarterback must place the ball. The reverse is true if the quarterback is on the back's right side. But the quarterback *must* be sure that it gets into that pocket, and the best way is to look right at the spot where he will place the ball. The runner won't be looking at the ball because he'll be searching for the opening in the line, or looking at his blockers or how the defense is reacting to him, so he depends totally on the quarterback putting the ball into that pocket.

There are other problems the quarterback has to overcome, and most of these are solved by the repetitions the offense makes in practice. Running backs come in all sizes, so the ball will not always land at the same spot if a

When he makes the handoff (photo 2-8), the quarterback must look at the pocket the runner has made with his hands and place the ball there and watch him grasp it.

quarterback just pivots and hands it off. That is why the quarterback must see the spot where he will place the ball and not allow it to bounce off a runner's chest or thighs. Some running backs get greedy and grab for the ball, but that tendency will lessen with work in practice. Some backs—O. J. Simpson was one—will take the ball with their hands and hold it against their stomach. That means the quarterback must place it right in the runner's hands and watch him grasp it.

Ninety-nine percent of fumbles on an exchange are caused by the quarterback not making the proper handoff, and most of these are because he did not watch where he placed the ball. Don't simply hold the ball out and take for granted that the back will get it. Fumbles from this kind of laziness are stupid because they are so elemental.

At the same time, a quarterback must not get too close to the back when he makes the handoff, but should give the runner as much room as possible to make his cuts where he sees an opening. This is best done by extending a bit to hand him the ball and always keeping it level with the QB's belt.

Since many high school and college quarterbacks work in the run-option system, such as the veer and wishbone, they also must be attentive to how they deliver the ball. Many times it won't happen until the last second because the quarterback might be reading a defensive end while moving along and holding the ball in the fullback's midsection. If he decides to hand it to the back, he cannot look for any pocket because he must concentrate on the defensive player's reaction, so it takes a keen understanding—a "feel" system—between the quarterback and the runner as to what will happen with the ball. This "feel" can only be developed in practice by constant repetition, but it is every bit as important as the straight handoff where the quarterback has "looked" the ball right into the back's hands.

There are three kinds of straight handoffs—the front out, the underneath and the reverse out, or pivot. The *front out* is simply moving to the right or left and handing off the ball. For instance, on a dive play to the right, the quarterback's first step is with the right foot down the line of scrimmage, or it may be backward for an off-tackle play from the I formation. I like this latter move because I tend to get the ball to the I formation back a bit deeper, and the deeper that he can get it in the backfield, the more time he has to read the line of scrimmage and find the best place to run. But in the front-out move, the first step always is in the direction in which the play is going.

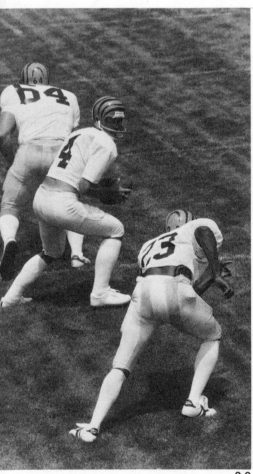

2-9   2-10   2-11

For the "front out" handoff, right or left, the quarterback takes one step toward the ball carrier while holding the ball at his belt (photo 2-9) and makes his next two steps as he places it into the runner's hands (photos 2-10, 2-11), then brings his feet together as the runner takes the ball and continues with his faking action (photos 2-12, 2-13).

2-12

2-13

41

The "underneath handoff" is used primarily for trap and misdirection plays. It starts as a front-out move (photos 2-14, 2-15), and then the quarterback starts backward and crosses the runner's path as he hands him the ball (photos 2-16, 2-17, 2-18), being careful to "look" it into the runner's hands.

The *underneath handoff* starts off like a front-out move, but it winds up with the quarterback handing the ball to his running back as the back is between him and the line of scrimmage. This means that the quarterback actually has crossed the path which the back will be taking toward the line, whereas in the other two handoffs, the quarterback is between the back and the line of scrimmage.

The back will start his run toward the right, and then cut back toward the left (or vice versa) as the quarterback takes the center's snap and begins his move backward. As the two cross paths, the quarterback then hands the ball forward, again being careful to actually look at the pocket the back has made to receive the ball before he gives it to him. This type of handoff is very effective with trap plays because the back can influence the defense to move in one direction, and then as he cuts back in the opposite tack and the defense turns to pursue, they are open to good blocking angles, which helps the offensive linemen spring some crunching trap blocks. Most of these plays are used with halfbacks whose speed is essential to come across the defense in the shortest possible time.

42

2-17

2-18

The "reverse out" or "pivot" handoff can go to the left or right. Here, I take the snap and pivot to my left (photos 2-19, 2-20), turning my back to the line of scrimmage (photo 2-21) before dealing the ball to the back as I did in the front-out move (photos 2-22, 2-23). Note I again look at the spot where the ball is being placed.

In the *reverse out* or *pivot*, the quarterback moves one way, then pivots and hands off the ball to a back coming from another direction. The quarterback will pivot on one foot and actually turn his back to the line of scrimmage while making his move. If the play goes to the left, he will reverse pivot on his left foot. This is a good example of "mentally" putting the weight on the left foot because he can plant that foot at the snap of the ball and reverse pivot around quickly to make a handoff.

The reverse pivot can be used for just about every play, from straight dives to counterplays. The series of runs that an offense decides to use will determine whether the quarterback will front out or reverse out in making his handoffs. Sometimes I'll front out on a play because we have both backs coming into the line and I'll hand it to the first one because it requires a quick move; then I might reverse out the next time to make the defense think I'm going to give the ball to the first back again. The front out is particularly useful for a quick-hitting type of play using an extremely quick back because the quarterback doesn't have time for an extra move.

Quite often the quarterback also must be just as quick in starting the series

45

of sweeps in his play repertoire. We call these "toss" plays because the quarterback will take the snap and toss it to a back running to the outside. The techniques are the same—take the ball, bring it into the stomach with both hands, pivot and then pitch it underhand from that position. Our quarterbacks are taught to throw the ball end over end to the back and just let him catch it. There are some quarterbacks—Joe Ferguson of the Buffalo Bills is one—who use an underhand spiral. I always felt the spiral was harder for the backs to catch, though Joe obviously never had any problems with O. J. Simpson when The Juice ran a sweep.

The method often boils down to individual coaching technique, but the key is that no matter how it's done, the ball must be delivered so the running back can catch it. It should be aimed in front of him, at his stomach or chest. If he has to jump for it, or reach behind or down to catch it, the play's timing will be destroyed. The toss play is most effective when you make the back stretch for the ball, which means he has to get out there under full power to make the catch. It doesn't matter if the toss is made from the front-out or reverse-out position, though we primarily use the latter. The follow-through is just as important here as in the inside handoff. The quarterback should be able to pitch the ball and continue on the same path. If the back does drop it or the pitch is off target, the quarterback is at least going in the right direction to make the recovery.

The eyes also are important because the quarterback has to pick out a point where he thinks the ball and back will intersect. During training camp, our quarterbacks and running backs have a little game on the toss play: we challenge them to reach our tosses, and they make the quarterbacks see how far they can pitch the ball. It develops some good habits because the play's key is getting outside before the defense can fully react.

It doesn't make any difference whether the quarterback is right- or left-handed when he makes the toss, because he must clutch the ball in both hands when he flips it. If I am going to toss it from the right, I'll reverse out to the left and flip it underhand. The problem for a quarterback using the spiral might come because he must get to a position where he won't have to

2-26

The "pitchout" or "toss" techniques start in the same manner as the other handoffs, with the ball grasped with both hands at the belt level. The quarterback pivots at a 45-degree angle and lowers the ball to get proper leverage (photo 2-24), and then tosses it underhand, end-over-end (photo 2-25), aiming it in front of the runner so he can catch it at his stomach or chest (photo 2-26). The quarterback must continue moving on the same path as the ball to complete the action.

underhand it across his body. Therefore, if he is right-handed and wants to toss to the left, he may front out and toss the ball; tossing to his right, he will either have to reverse out to free his arm or front out and add a backward step to get free, taking time and possibly altering the angle of his toss.

Regardless of whether the quarterback uses the front-out or reverse-pivot handoff, he still must be capable of executing creditable fakes to his running backs—that is, making a move with the ball as if to hand it to one back, then pulling it back and giving it to a second back. There was a time in pro football when teams placed a great premium on this kind of deception, and I've often heard Paul Brown talk about Frank Albert and Eddie LeBaron, and the absolute wizardry they displayed with their ball-handling techniques. Coach Brown said it often was impossible to find the ball when they went to work with their fakes. In my time, Steve Grogan, Bob Griese and Joe Theismann are three of the best I've seen.

Pro football, at least, has changed in the respect that there aren't fancy running games anymore. Everyone has huge linemen and there is a lot of straight-ahead blocking to blow out the defense and carve out big holes for the running backs. Washington certainly displayed that in Super Bowl XVII. The "Hogs," its offensive line, simply blew down the Dolphins' defense. Also, with so many teams using single setback formations, the need for faking lessens because there isn't anyone to fake to. Certainly, if you have a back like Marcus Allen or O. J. Simpson, just get him the ball and let him make his own moves.

The techniques for faking and handing off are the same as for the straight handoff—have the ball secured in both hands, fake it, pull it back and then hand it off, all on a motion from belt level. The key is to make the first move look like an actual handoff so it must be as realistic as possible, which is why the technique must be the same as if the play was a straight handoff.

The same commandments hold for the various uses of the fake—draw plays and play-action passes. The draw play is effective only if the passing game is an integral part of the offense, and is particularly useful when the pass rush is beginning to heat up. Sting the opposition's front a couple of

47

times and they'll be more cautious, which means an additional second or more for the quarterback to throw the ball.

There are three different kinds of draw plays, all of which *must* be disguised as potential pass plays to be effective:

1. The quarterback brings the ball back to a stationary running back who is posing as a blocker, and hands it to him. The back then will take off from that standing position.

2. The quarterback brings the ball back and hands it to a back who has begun to move forward.

3. The quarterback drops back as if to pass, going slightly beyond a stationary back. He then will step forward and hand the ball to the back. We call this an "enema draw," and the theory behind it is that once the quarterback passes the running back, the defense will believe that the threat of a run is gone and it will immediately play for a pass.

The draw play and the play-action pass (which we'll discuss later in more detail) that comes off the fake draw play are good weapons in forcing a de-

2-27

2-28

2-30

2-31

fense to hesitate getting into its coverage. The key in "selling" the draw play is the quarterback keeping his eyes focused downfield as if he was reading the pass coverage. That gets a bit scary sometimes because he knows he must hand off the ball somewhere behind him and he can't turn around and look for the back because that will blow the deception. The longer he keeps his eyes looking downfield before making the forward handoff, the better off he'll be. The running back must get into the right position for that handoff, and it is the quarterback's responsibility to "look" the handoff into the back's hands. This is a rather delicate operation because of that dual responsibility, so both players have to be sure they have the play timed to perfection during the week's practice sessions.

One last point on faking the handoff: If the quarterback wants to be successful with play-action passing, after every running play he should continue his fake so that when he does use a play-action pass, his motion will be the same and a defense that has been used to seeing him follow through with those fakes may be fooled on this sequence. Faking after handing off is one

2-29

The "draw play" must begin as if it were going to be a pass and the quarterback must "sell" that idea with his eyes looking downfield for a receiver as he comes away from the center (photos 2-27, 2-28). He brings the ball to the back who moves to a position to receive it (photo 2-29) before moving forward. The quarterback must again look at the spot where he places the ball (photo 2-30) and continue back as if he were going to pass (photos 2-31, 2-32).

2-32

49

area that I have to work on because in the past our system did not feature a lot of play-action passing, and partly too because I tend to stand there and look around a little bit after I hand off the ball instead of continuing my part of the action to the very end. If it can happen to someone who has played the game for nearly twenty years, then young quarterbacks can see the danger of slipping into the same bad habits.

That may seem like a minor point but that good fake may fool only one player—the one who would make the tackle. Every detail in a play is important for its success.

Chapter 3
The Drop-Back and Passing

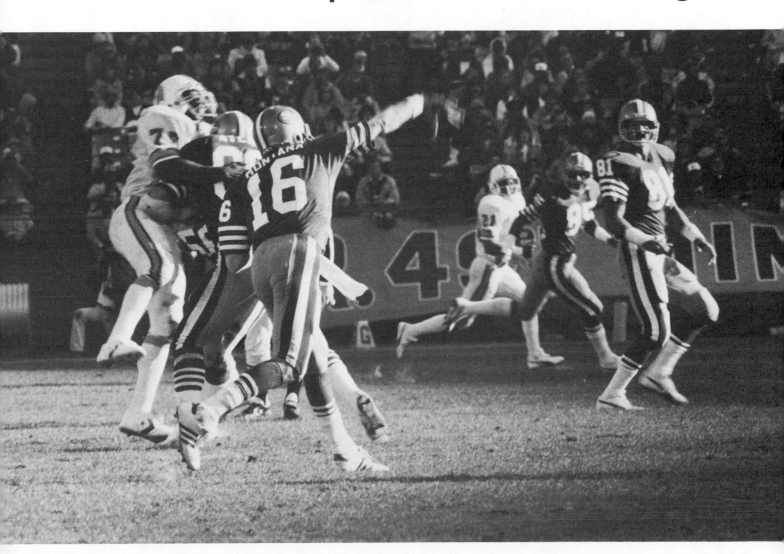

PROFESSIONAL football always has put a great premium on a quarterback who is an outstanding passer, and now that the passing game is gaining prominence at the intercollegiate and high school levels, no quarterback can afford to overlook any of the techniques that are important to this phase of playing the position. As I noted, when I came to the Bengals I literally started from scratch to learn the proper techniques and I had a fine position coach in Bill Walsh, who has had great success as head coach at Stanford and later with the San Francisco 49ers. He was not only a fine teacher but an excellent technician who stressed every nuance and forced me to pay the same close attention.

I know that sitting in the stands or watching a game on television doesn't really do justice to all of the technical elements a quarterback must perfect in his passing game because everything seems to happen so fast. But then, all of this is like walking or running: each muscle movement determines the next, and taken together, they produce an action that is so automatic. A quarterback's action in passing the football must be just as automatic, but at the same time, it must have a precision that will allow him to deliver the ball from any different number of positions and under all kinds of circumstances. He cannot be thinking about the technical elements as he prepares to throw, because from the time that he takes the snap from center until he delivers the ball, he has, at most, three or four seconds to get the job done. Therefore, his mental energies must be pointed in only one direction: getting the ball to an open receiver.

Before he can do that, there are a number of technical checkpoints which must be ticked off in rapid fashion, beginning with the position of his feet as he stands behind the center awaiting the snap. This is not any different than if he is going to hand off the ball for a run because, as we noted in the last chapter, he cannot tip off the play by radically altering his foot position. This sounds simple but I used to get into trouble at times because my first step away from center was not always precise and I got stepped on. There wasn't any time to try to correct a bad habit in the middle of the season so I went to a slight cheat step—placing the right, or getaway, foot slightly behind my left foot. I find now that it has helped me make a cleaner getaway.

I do not advocate this for every quarterback. The ideal stance still is with the feet parallel, shoulder width apart, and knees slightly flexed, and then using the proper foot movement to get back into a throwing position. As a quarterback gets more experience, he can alter these things to where he will

53

be most comfortable, but for those who are just starting out, I suggest that they master the basics first. It well may be that their footwork will be so adept that they never will have to change, and that's all right, too.

Either way, the quarterback's weight should be on the balls of both feet until he shouts out the signal on which the ball is to be snapped. At that instant, the weight is shifted onto the left foot (reversed for lefties), and that involves what I referred to earlier as "mentally" placing weight on that foot as you anticipate the snap count; when the ball is centered you lift the right foot to begin a backward move. Before I went to a slight cheat step, I dropped my butt as soon as I took the snap because something had to get me started backward. That isn't a bad technique for quarterbacks who assume the parallel stance; for those who use the slight cheat step, this already has the quarterback started to his drop area.

In taking the snap, the quarterback and center must spend enough time working together—just the two of them if necessary—so that the ball's laces will hit the fingers of the right hand (or left hand for left-handed throwers) at the snap, giving the quarterback the ball in a position to throw it even before he leaves the area. This is most important when the quarterback wants to throw the quick rhythm pass, where he moves just a step or two then straightens up and throws. He won't have time to adjust the ball in these one-second passes, so he must have the proper grip from the moment he grasps the ball.

Once the quarterback gets the ball, he must bring it into his stomach to protect it, just as he does before handing it off on a running play. Then, as he turns to drop back, he should bring it to a position in front of his chest, holding it with both hands. Often quarterbacks will drop back or sprint out with the ball held in a very high position, often around their ear. I find this difficult for me because I don't feel comfortable as I move. With the ball at chest level, my arms can swing freely, and this doesn't hinder the quickness that is so necessary in getting to my drop area. Of course, this is also a coaching technique and there are coaches who prefer that their quarterbacks hold the ball high as they drop back, so the quarterback must adhere to his coach's wishes.

But regardless of how the quarterback holds the ball, he really can do nothing with it until he sets up properly to pass. This means getting to his drop position as quickly as possible. Here a quarterback's foot speed is the key, because he only has a few seconds in which to pass, so the quicker he gets into position to throw, the more he will be able to see and the sooner he can take advantage of the defense. So often you see quarterbacks being sacked and their offensive line gets criticized, when in reality the quarterback himself has been lazy or slow in setting up, and then he tries to do everything as if he still had all the time in the world. Joe Namath was a good example of a quarterback who was almost perfect in this move. He would sprint away from the center, like a spring uncoiling, and he was back to his drop point in no more than a second.

The speed of a quarterback's drop is tied into the kind of drop that he prefers. There are two: (1) the turn and move and (2) the backpedal. Most quarterbacks, myself included, use the *turn and move*. The technique is to turn half of your body—the side opposite your throwing arm—away from the center of the field and sprint back to the spot where you will throw the ball, then square away and set up to pass. A quarterback using this style will reach that spot quicker than if he backpedaled, but he'll have seen only half the field en route, so he then must check the other half.

This isn't as difficult or as time-consuming as it may seem, and much depends on the particular pass pattern. If it is a deeper pattern, I always read the coverage down the center of the field as I sprint back. I basically will know where the defensive people should be, and once I reach the spot where I will set up and pass, I can confirm that coverage and then pick up my receivers. If the pattern is to be quick, the ball to be thrown off the third or fifth step, I use the same turn-and-move technique but I still won't throw blindly. I must know the position of the linebacker on the side where the ball is going, so as soon as I turn I try to pick him up and then pick out my receiver. We'll discuss these various passing positions in more detail later in this chapter.

For a quarterback using the *backpedal movement*—Dan Fouts of the San Diego Chargers and Earl Morrall, who played for nineteen seasons in the NFL and won three Super Bowl rings, mastered it—there is the advantage of seeing all of the field as he moves so he will be set to throw as soon as he arrives at his drop spot. He will also spot any blitzing linebackers or defensive backs from either side of the defense, whereas the turn-and-move quarterback is nearly blind to the side opposite the ball until he sets up to throw. Then it is often too late; other times he must hurry his throw or, hopefully, spot the blitz before the ball is snapped. The disadvantage that I see in the backpedal is not getting enough depth in the pass drop nor getting there as quickly as with the turn and move, but that didn't inhibit either Dan or Earl.

In fact, I have tried to incorporate some of the backpedal into my own style, because it is effective on certain types of passes. But because I never worked at it extensively, I've found it very awkward and I couldn't do it on a full-time basis. Yet, as I noted, you can't argue with the success that others have had using it.

All of our discussions about the various types of pass drops will be centered about the turn-and-move technique. The first is the *straight drop-back* where a quarterback moves directly into a protective pocket formed by his linemen. The depth of that drop, or the number of steps the quarterback will use to get there, falls into three categories:

3-1

3-2

Dan Fouts of the San Diego Chargers begins his backpedal move, stepping with his right foot first after taking the snap (photo 3-1). As he continues to step backward, he is looking at his receivers and the defensive coverage (photos 3-2 through 3-6). When he reaches his set point, he sets up and is prepared to deliver the ball (photos 3-7, 3-8, 3-9).

3-6

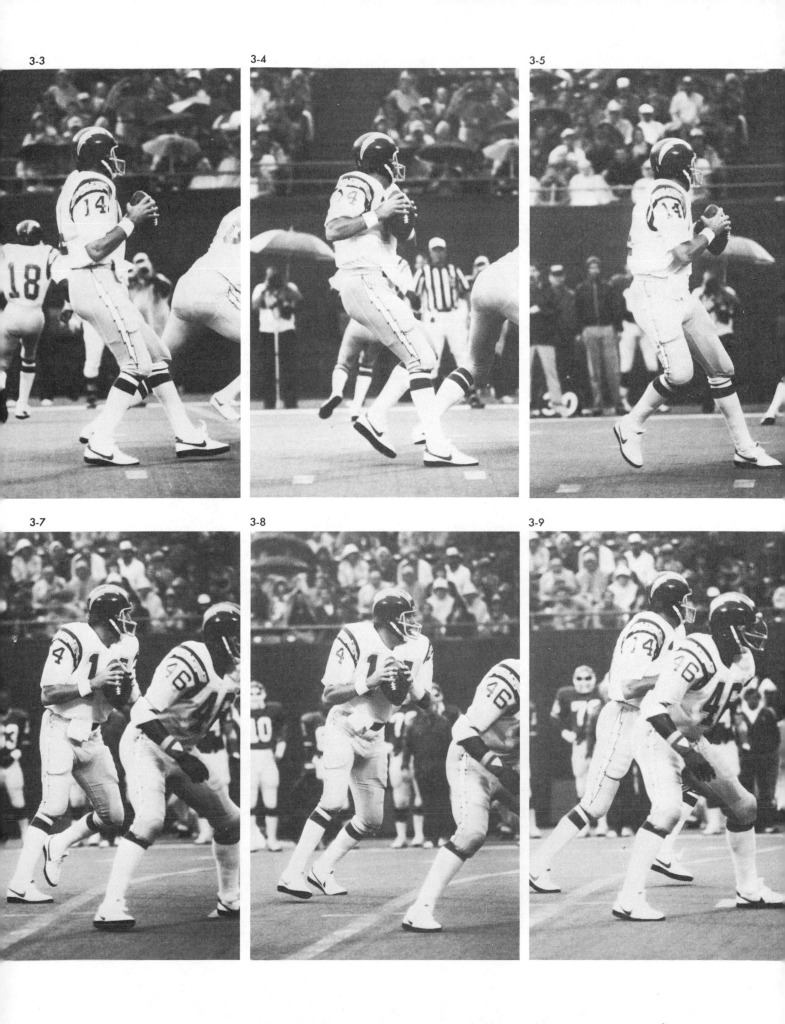

3-3

3-4

3-5

3-7

3-8

3-9

1. *Three-step drop*:   The key is to take those three steps as quickly as possible, because the patterns used in this maneuver generally are the little quick "out" passes and the "slant" patterns over the middle. The three steps will carry the quarterback about four yards behind his center and he must then step up and throw. He should remember that his offensive line will be using the "cut" technique in their blocking—trying to knock the defensive people off their feet so they can't raise their arms to block the pass. Balls thrown from this limited depth have a much straighter trajectory so the passer must have clear lanes. If he waits too long, the defense can recover and either throw up a wall of hands and arms or, worse yet, sack him.

The three-step pass drop must be done quickly and the three steps (photos 3-11, 3-14, 3-17) will carry the quarterback four yards behind his center, where he then sets up to throw (photos 3-18 through 3-20) and finishes his move by stepping up as he throws the ball (photos 3-25, 3-26).

3-13

3-14

3-10

3-11

3-12

3-15

3-16

3-17

3-18

3-19

3-22

3-23

3-20

3-21

3-24

3-25

3-26

2. *Five-step drop:* This is tied in with medium-range passes where the quarterback sprints back five steps (six or seven yards) and is ready to throw on that fifth step. A quarterback needs a strong arm to work from this drop because many ten- or twelve-yard "out" patterns utilize this technique, so the ball must be thrown with good velocity but without the luxury of having time to wind up and let it go. It is particularly important here that a quarterback not have any lazy habits in getting into the pocket and being ready to throw.

3-27   3-28   3-29   3-30

3-35   3-36   3-37   3-38

The five-step pass drop brings the quarterback six or seven yards behind the center with large, comfortable steps (photos 3-30, 3-34, 3-37, 3-38, 3-40) and with his body perpendicular to the line of scrimmage. That final step brings him to a position to set up quickly (photos 3-43 through 3-50). This drop often is used for high-velocity passes that are thrown without winding up.

3-31	3-32	3-33	3-34

3-39	3-40	3-41	3-42

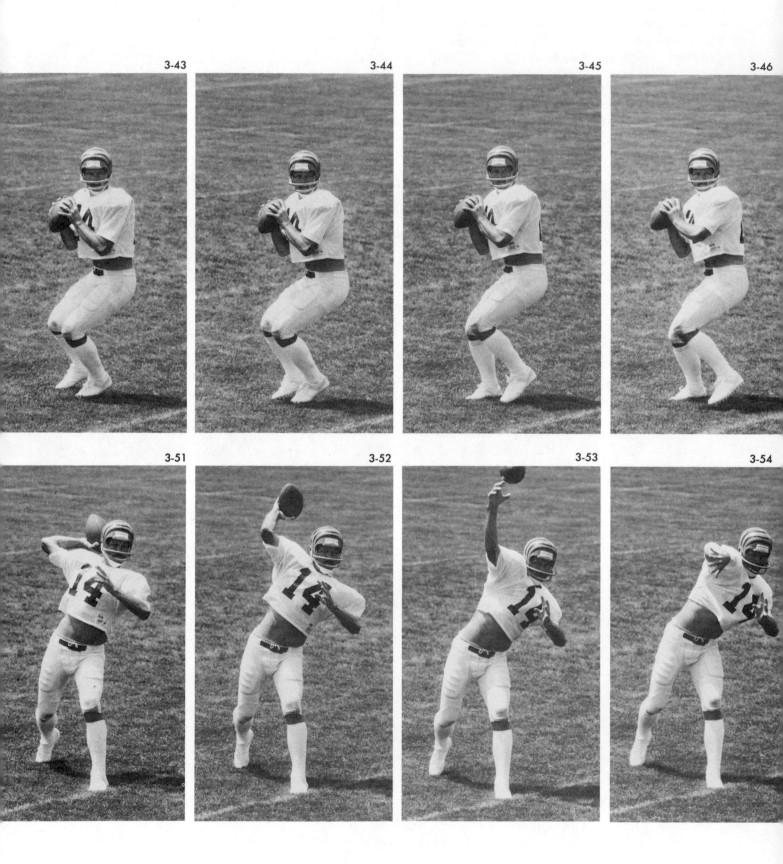

3-43 3-44 3-45 3-46

3-51 3-52 3-53 3-54

3-47   3-48   3-49   3-50

3-55   3-56

3. *Seven-step drop:* This is the conventional pass drop of nine or ten yards. The quarterback must stay in control of his body on this move so his first four steps backward should be longer than the last three, to get him sufficient depth; the last three can be shorter so that he gets the proper balance that will bring him to the correct throwing position. On the seventh step, he should be able to bounce forward to that position. Stepping forward is important because the offensive linemen are taught to try to move the outside pass rushers around the quarterback, thus forming a protective cup from which he can operate. The passer can help his linemen by stepping up and out of the line in which these defenders are being pushed. I learned the hard way a couple of years ago because I was hitting my set point and then actually retreating a yard farther backward. I was getting sacked a lot and the offensive line was getting criticized when they really were doing their job. The quarterback must hit that set point, and then shuffle up into the pocket as he takes his step to throw the ball.

The seven-step pass drop is used for most medium- and long-range patterns, and carries the quarterback about nine or ten yards behind his center. His first four steps (photos 3-58, 3-61, 3-65, 3-69) should be longer to get him proper depth as quickly as possible;

3-57

3-58

3-63

3-64

3-65

3-66

3-59   3-60   3-61   3-62

3-67   3-68   3-69   3-70

and the last three steps (photos 3-71, 3-75, 3-77) shorter, with his body tilted slightly backward to help him regain his balance for the correct throwing position. On the seventh step he must bounce forward to that position (photos 3-77, 3-78, 3-79).

3-71

3-72

3-77

3-78

3-79

3-80

3-85

3-86

3-87

3-88

| 3-73 | 3-74 | 3-75 | 3-76 |

| 3-81 | 3-82 | 3-83 | 3-84 |

3-89   3-90

69

Now a tip on the turn-and-move technique for these drops: If I am committed to throw to my left—the side away from my vision as I drop back—rather than having my hips perpendicular to the line of scrimmage, I'll keep them at a 45-degree angle as I move because that allows more of my vision to be focused to the left. This is particularly important for the five-step drop because I must check the coverage before throwing the "out" pass to prevent it from being picked off and run in for a score. In the seven-step drop, the hips are more perpendicular to the line of scrimmage because your vision widens to the left side of the field on those last three steps. Of course, a commitment to throw to the right means not having to worry because that portion of the field is visible as you drop back.

The next kind of pass is the *fake and drop back,* or the *play-action pass,* in which the quarterback will pretend to hand the ball to a back as if he had called a running play, and then drop to a point and throw a pass. This always is an effective weapon when a team's running game is going well and the defense, particularly the linebackers, are concentrating on getting to the runners. It also is a good play on some third-down situations where a run is the logical play to try to get a first down. In either instance, if the linebackers follow the running back after the fake, the quarterback will have more room for his receivers; and even if the linebackers don't totally bite, those couple of moments' hesitation can be enough to get a receiver behind them and into the open.

So often you see quarterbacks doing what I call the "lazy man's fake"—that is, they will stick an empty hand into the runner's stomach and keep the ball cradled by their chest. Why, I even remember a picture on the cover of *Sports Illustrated* many years ago which showed one of college football's great quarterbacks at that time making such a move.

That really doesn't fool anyone. The defense easily can see that he isn't getting the ball so they don't even bother to react. The quarterback actually must stick the ball in front of the runner's pocket with the same motion that he uses on all of his handoffs, and he must allow the defense to see it heading there, before he pulls it back. This is an art and it requires a lot of work, plus the coordination of both the runner and the offensive line. Once the quarterback has taken the ball back on the fake, the runner has to keep going aggressively to the line of scrimmage just as if he had the ball. He can't make the play with both arms pumping, nor can he pull up and stop once he passes the quarterback, because the defense will spot the fake instantly and still be able to get back to protect against the pass.

Offensive linemen are taught to be passive—that is, to step back—in their pass protection blocking, so it is against their nature to fire out on a pass play. For one thing, they take great pride in protecting the quarterback and an aggressive block is not the best kind for defeating a pass rush. Yet on a play-action pass, the line must make its blocks as if the play is a run because linebackers are very keen in picking up the slightest difference in a blocking scheme. If they see a lineman step back, even though a runnning back is coming their way, they will know immediately that the play is going to be a pass and disregard the play-action aspects.

For the quarterback, the important thing is that he must know the point where he will set up to pass. He may start going straight backward but, after making his fake, wind up behind the guard's position. If that is how the play is designed, then that is the point the line will be protecting, and they will expect him to be there. It doesn't matter whether the quarterback is dropping straight back, sprinting out or faking in a semisprint (all of which we'll discuss shortly), he *must* be in the position where the linemen expect him to be. Blocking schemes are drawn up precisely to take advantage of these kinds of moves, and if the quarterback winds up over the tackle or behind the center when he should be behind the guard, then he has defeated that scheme all by himself.

There are other key points to remember in using play-action passes:

1. Single-setback formations are not ideal for such maneuvers because you won't fool many people about your intentions.

2. These plays start out looking like successful running plays. Defenses pick up tendencies from their film study, such as knowing that a team always runs a play-action pass from a particular movement by the backs. The actual running play and play-action pass must look identical to be effective. Remember, too, that a couple of successful play-action passes also can lull the linebackers so they might hesitate on their run coverage just long enough for a back to burst through the line and make some good yardage.

3. It doesn't make any sense to use play-action passes in long-yardage situations. When it's a third-and-twelve, the defense knows you are looking for a first down and that you will have the best chance of achieving it by throwing the ball, so it will simply disregard any play-action fakes and immediately play pass defense. It would be better to get that back quickly into a pass pattern and force extra coverage, perhaps opening some space for another receiver.

An offshoot of the play-action pass is the *fake and sprint out*, where a quarterback is trying to break the containment tactics of the defensive end or linebacker by getting outside them as quickly as possible and then setting up to throw, throw on the run or just take off and run with the ball. Quarterbacks must challenge the line of scrimmage and run with the ball occasionally to make the defense worry about the three options. If it fears his running and comes up, he can throw over it while still on the move, a technique we'll discuss shortly; if the defense lays back, then he can take off with the ball.

But before all of this happens, the fake to the running back must be convincing enough to occupy the defensive end and linebacker and get them moving toward him, and in an opposite direction to his own path. This will give him some wide open spaces from which to operate.

The sprint-out pass works best with the quarterback looking as if he is challenging the line of scrimmage because he cannot stop to throw. Thus, he must rotate his hips and move his shoulders to face the target (photos 3-91, 3-92, 3-93) and then continue on the same path as the ball (photo 3-94, 3-95). When moving to the left, he also must open his hips (photo 3-96) and get his right shoulder facing the target (3-97).

The semisprint pass drop often follows a fake handoff, and then the quarterback moves quickly to a spot five yards behind the offensive tackle. He must set up quickly (photos 3-99, 3-100) and assume a good throwing position (3-101, 3-102) because he will throw as soon as he arrives at his set point.

3-99

3-100

3-101

An offshoot of this play is the *fake handoff and semisprint,* a move that can get the quarterback to the right or to the left with almost equal facility. This really is the "moving-pocket" technique where the quarterback will set up to pass in different positions behind his line and thus take away from the defense the idea that it can target one particular area for blitzes or other stunts by its linemen. Again, the linemen expect him to arrive at a specific spot, and they will work to protect that area, so his move must be precise. Moving to the right does not pose much of a problem for me, as a right-handed thrower, because I'll arrive in position to throw the ball. Moving to the left requires more adjustment because I'll get there with the left side of my body fully open in that direction, so I must plant my left foot and then quickly make a hop-step turn to get my body facing downfield and my shoulders, hips and legs lined up and facing my target. Of course, the opposite moves are in effect for the left-handed thrower.

These motions are equally important when quarterbacks utilize the *roll-out pass.* Whether he sprints out or rolls out, the quarterback must have his shoulders facing his target. On the roll out, unlike the other passes we've dis-

3-102

3-103

75

cussed, no faking is involved, so it normally is a committed move from the snap of the ball. The key to success is that the quarterback should be able to throw and continue to run on the same path that the ball is traveling and even pick it up if he ever has to. Thus the importance of the position of the shoulders.

A quarterback can't be running to his right, parallel to the line of scrimmage, and throw across his body because he won't get anything on the ball. Even though his legs are carrying him in that direction, he still must rotate

3-104

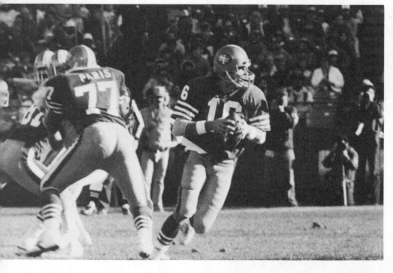

3-105

3-108

3-109

3-112

3-113

his hips and thus move his shoulders toward the target. Running to the left—if he is a right-handed thrower—means that the quarterback must open his hips more to get his right shoulder in position to face his target. When I was at Augustana, I could execute these moves with great facility, but in the pros we don't throw as much on the run and I've gotten away from some of the techniques, though I've begun trying to sharpen them again, because defenses have become so sophisticated that they force a passer to utilize many different styles.

3-106

3-107

3-110

3-111

3-114

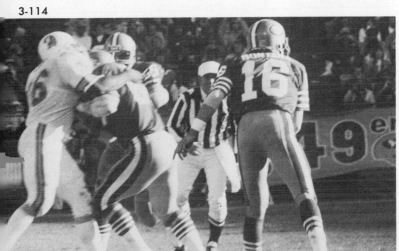

Joe Montana of the 49ers executes a perfect roll-out pass as he takes the snap and heads away from the center in a 45-degree angle to his right (photos 3-104 through 3-108). He then continues his path to the spot where he will throw the ball, always staying within the protection pattern designed for the play (photos 3-108, 3-109, 3-110). As he prepares to deliver the ball, he squares his shoulders to face his target (photos 3-111, 3-112) and then delivers the ball in perfect form (photos 3-113, 3-114).

3-115

In the second sequence, Joe demonstrates the effectiveness of the roll-out pass near the goal line by moving to spread the defense and make it play the option of pass or run (photos 3-115, 3-116, 3-117). When he sees his receivers covered, he then has a convoy of blockers for his run to the end zone (photo 3-118, 3-120).

3-118

3-116

3-117

3-119

3-120

79

And in throwing on the run, *do not* try to lead your receiver with the ball. Instead, throw the ball right at his body because both of you are moving at the same pace and your body's momentum will naturally take the ball in front of him to make the catch. If you try to lead him, he will never catch up with the ball. You also must follow through as you would if you were throwing from a stationary position to keep the ball from sailing over the receiver's head. As we will discuss shortly, the follow-through will bring the ball on a downward path. You need not worry about velocity because, as you throw on the run, the movement of your body produces a great deal more momentum for the ball than if you were standing still. If the receiver is close to you, take something off the ball and give him a chance to catch it.

Ever since the Dallas Cowboys began using it about ten years ago, more and more teams have installed the *shotgun formation* for use on obvious third-down passing situations. Coach Tom Landry of the Cowboys merely borrowed a page from a very old playbook that he carried when he was a player for the New York Giants and resurrected the old A formation, a form of the double wing in which the quarterback lines up seven yards behind the center much as the tailback did in those old formations. He doesn't try to

3-121

3-122

3-125

3-126

Danny White of the Cowboys sets up in the shotgun formation by standing five yards behind his center (photo 3-121). As soon as the ball reaches his hands, he begins his pass drop (photos 3-122, 3-123, 3-124) and scans the defense as his receivers run their routes (photos 3-125 through 3-128).

3-123

3-124

3-127

3-128

Danny uses the same sidestep motion to reach his drop point as he does in his normal drop-back method, the difference being that he goes only five more yards (photos 3-129 through 3-132) before setting up and preparing to throw (photos 3-133 through 3-139).

3-129

3-132

3-133

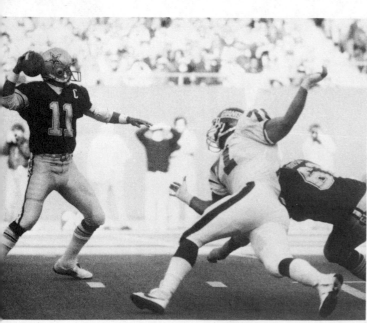

3-136

3-137

3-130

3-131

3-134

3-135

3-138

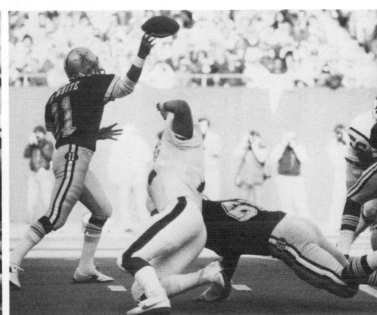

3-139

fool anyone, though the Cowboys do use more running plays from it than other teams, because the idea is for the quarterback to see everything in front of him as the ball is being centered, while also having the advantage of getting more time to select a receiver by not having to drop back. Roger Staubach and now Danny White have been very successful running it for the Cowboys, and that success has emboldened others, at all levels, to install it.

We even used it a few years ago in one game against the Los Angeles Rams, which at the time featured a lot of blitzing by their safeties. We used our two running backs, set alongside me, to form a blocking screen to pick them up. I found that I still preferred the turn and drop-back move because, in the shotgun, I concentrated first on catching the long center snap and then had to look for the defensive coverage. When I took the normal center snap, I could read the coverages quicker because I could see half the field as I hustled back to set up, and quickly checked the other coverages before throwing.

The shotgun certainly is a coaching prerogative and it requires a quarterback who is sure-handed and a center who can make a long snap without looking at his target. This means the quarterback should get the ball at chest level so that he can immediately get it into the passing position, but if snaps come lower or higher he also must be deft enough to snare them and quickly be ready to throw. Danny White was a great infielder at Arizona State, and that certainly shows when he is forced to field some errant snaps. Me? I don't know.

Adherents of the shotgun point out the advantages of being able to scan the field from the snap of the ball. That is something that every quarterback must do, regardless of the kind of pass he is going to throw and from where he is throwing it. On every pattern, the quarterback will have a progression list of receivers to whom he can look and, as we noted before, that can be discarded if, when he is calling signals, he sees one totally uncovered. All he does then is throw him the ball.

What a quarterback looks for as he scans depends on down and distance. If it is first-and-ten and the first receiver in my progression list is open on a four- or five-yard pattern, I will throw him the ball right away. Sometimes the armchair quarterbacks will see another receiver break into the clear on that play and they will grouse that the quarterback missed a touchdown. Here, it gets to be a matter of philosophy. Ours is to control the ball by completing a high percentage of our passes, and that means being willing to take the short ones rather than waiting for the longer ones to come open on the early downs. The Raiders and Steelers are teams that prefer to get something big with most of their throws, so their quarterbacks may pass up the short gain in favor of something deeper.

Now if it's third-and-ten, I'm not going to take a four-yard receiver unless I absolutely have to because I want the first down. Therefore, as the quarterback scans the field, his offensive philosophy will dictate what he will do; he will also recognize what the defense is allowing him to do and what the capabilities of his receivers are against these defensive maneuvers. We'll discuss in greater detail some of these strategic elements later in the book, but for now it suffices to say that when the quarterback scans the field, he should know what he is looking for, and then go after it by using any of the various means we have just discussed.

Having made his pass drop and scanned the field, the quarterback now is ready to throw the ball. This is an action that encompasses the coordination of the hand, shoulders, right elbow, arm, hips, and feet, all working together in a marvelous symmetry that produces automatic weight transfer from one part of the body to the next as part of a throwing motion that I never really studied in any detail until I began preparing the material for this book.

Throwing a football is much like tying a necktie: you do it so automatically that when someone asks you to break down the process on a step-by-step basis, you simply are unable to do so unless you are watching yourself in slow motion. I brought out a home video camera and had pictures taken as I threw the ball no more than fifteen yards just so I could study the physiological elements of the process. I also watched the process by which I get the ball into the throwing position and how I grip it prior to its release.

Here is what I found that would be applicable to a right-handed quarterback:

Getting the Ball into the Throwing Position: As we have discussed, the ball should be carried with both hands until the quarterback reaches the spot where he will throw it. It then should be pushed backward with the left hand, a motion that will raise it upward and into a position behind the head where it can be cocked and ready to be released.

Grip: This is a very individual thing and I don't think any NFL quarterback does it similarly. One of our former coaches, George Sefcik, once clipped from various magazines pictures of quarterbacks holding the football in the throwing position, and of the two dozen or so photos, there weren't two passers holding the ball the same way. Terry Bradshaw, for example, will keep the index finger of his throwing hand on the rear tip of the ball before he throws; other passers will have their hands near the middle of the ball.

The determining factor is hand size. The bigger your hand, the closer to the center of the ball you may wish to place it. The important thing is to have at least one finger on the laces. As the illustrations show, I grip a football by placing my little finger and my right ring finger on the laces of the

3-140   3-141

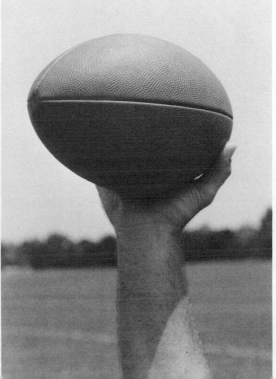

In gripping the ball to throw, the bigger the quarterback's hand, the closer to the center of the ball he should place it and have at least one finger on the laces. I place my index finger on the seams and my middle, ring and little fingers on the laces; and my thumb acts as a support (photo 3-140). The ball should be gripped by the fingertips and not rest in the palm of the hand (photo 3-141) to produce a good overhand spiral.

ball. The middle finger and the index finger are ahead of the laces and on the seams, and my thumb acts as a support beneath the ball. The thumb is so overlooked in importance but a broken bone in the thumb area is a debilitating injury for a quarterback because it is impossible for him to grip the ball without using it.

Quarterbacks should not have a death grip on the ball, but rather more of a fingertip grip that keeps it from resting in the palm of the hand. If the palm is on the ball, there is a tendency to throw with more of a sidearm motion because the ball must come off the palm rather than roll off the fingers, lessening the tendency to spiral the ball or get the proper follow-through. Throwing the ball off the fingers allows for a pure overhand motion, a proper follow-through and subsequently a good spiral, so necessary for keeping the ball in the air the minimum amount of time.

The throwing motion begins with the proper grip (photo 3-142). The ball is pushed into position (photos 3-143, 3-144, 3-145) and the right, or rear, leg is firmly planted (photos 3-146, 3-147).

3-142

3-143

3-144

Throwing the Ball: There is a six-step sequence, and our directions here are for right-handed passers. Lefties can simply apply the opposite side of their body. The sequence goes like this:

1. Grip the ball properly.

2. Push the ball into the throwing position.

3. The weight then is totally on the right side, resting on the right, or rear, leg, which is firmly planted.

4. The weight transfer, which provides the power for the throw, begins with the left leg lifted slightly and the left arm moving toward the target. This will open up the left hip, so important for accuracy, because the passer must face the person to whom he is throwing.

5. As the ball is cocked to be thrown, the right elbow will lead the way as the forward arm motion begins with the right wrist firmly locked.

6. The weight transfer will be completed with the left foot on the ground as the right wrist and forearm catch up with the hips and the ball is released just past the head. We have illustrated all of these steps in intricate detail on these pages.

3-145

3-146

3-147

The left leg is slightly lifted and the left arm moves toward the target, opening up the left hip and transferring the weight (photos 3-148, 3-149). As the ball is cocked to throw, the right elbow leads the way and the right wrist is locked (photos 3-150, 3-151). The ball is released just past the head (photo 3-152), and the weight transfer is completed with the left foot on the ground as the right wrist and forearm catch up with the hips (photos 3-153, 3-154). The throwing motion must bring the arm down across the body with the wrist leading the way after having been snapped by the ball's release (photos 3-155, 3-156, 3-157).

3-148

3-152

3-153

3-154

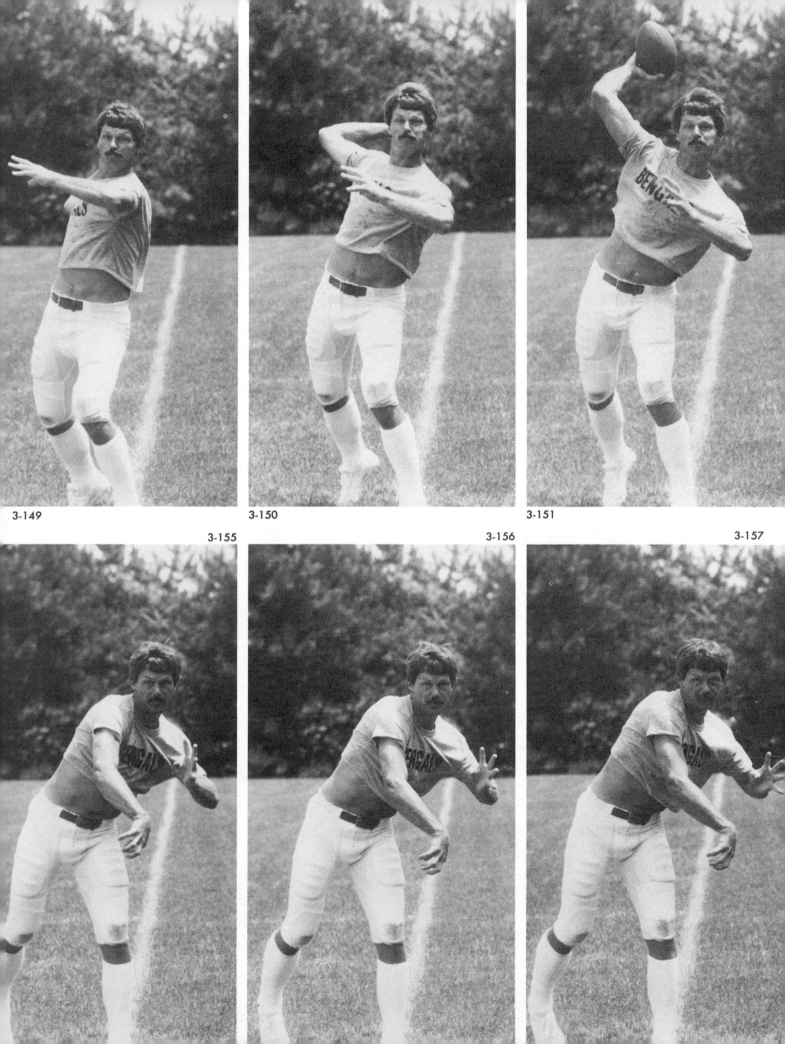

3-149

3-150

3-151

3-155

3-156

3-157

What the passer does next is equally important to the manner in which he has just delivered the ball. If the ball is to be thrown low, it should be released a fraction of a second later than for a ball that needs more arc to cover a greater distance. That timing takes care of the nose of the ball, a sort of propeller that takes it from the release point and toward the receiver.

Now comes the follow-through, whose importance we mentioned earlier, and this is achieved by continuing the throwing arm straight downward. The momentum from its swing will bring the arm across the body in a very natural motion. The key here is not to make it a conscious move, lest you interrupt the natural flow. Almost imperceptible in this process is the right wrist, which actually leads the way and is turned, or snapped, by the ball as it is released. In looking at my own throwing motion on a frame-by-frame breakdown, I saw that my wrist actually did snap downward. This gave the ball its tight spiral motion and helped to propel my arm on its downward follow-through course. This also brought my body into a squared-up position with the path of the ball and the receiver.

Since most passes are thrown from this position, these are the basic motions that I find to be the most important for achieving overall passing success. But there also are many variations to this theme, and we'll discuss those in the next chapter.

Chapter 4
Types of Passes and When to Throw Them

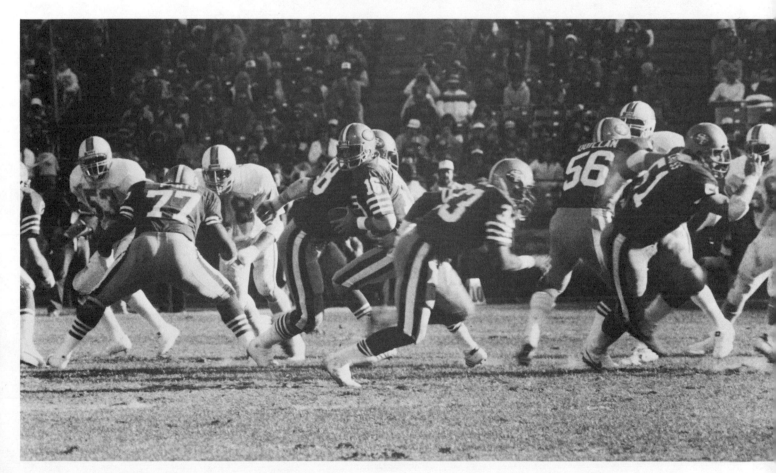

DESPITE all of the gaudy statistics that have been accumulated in the National Football League over the past few seasons, passing the football successfully is not the by-product of some mad genius who sits up nights concocting mind-boggling plays. Believe it or not, there are only eleven basic pass patterns, and that includes two we call the hitch and post-corner, which are variations of other pass routes. The screen pass, which is a specially designed play, has no specific route. We have diagramed what is called a "passing tree," which illustrates all but the screen pass. The difference in

THE PASSING TREE

The Passing Tree, with the various routes appearing as branches. Note that the hook and comeback patterns both work off the streak; and the post-corner features a 90-degree turn off the normal post pattern. Obviously, these routes can be run in opposite directions simply by turning the tree around.

some teams being more successful with them than other teams is how and when they are used—and perhaps most importantly how they are *not* used. Like everything else in football, a system can be successful if all that is designed for it makes sense, if it is capable of working, and if the people who must make it work can understand and acknowledge its limitations.

All of this falls under the category of constructing a pass offense philosophy. As we noted in the last chapter, ours in Cincinnati differs from that of other teams in the league. That is not to say that ours is the best and the only one to use. It is the one that has been successful for us because it fits the talent of our passers, our receivers, and the manner in which our coaches feel we can best attack the defenses that are prevalent in professional football.

Of course, other teams have different kinds of personnel and a different approach to the same problems, and many of them are successful because their people can do some things that ours cannot do. Hence, they can make the Xs and Os their coaches draw on the board come alive in a different way. As I noted earlier, Terry Bradshaw, for example, always had a stronger arm than I do, so he can afford to wait for deeper patterns to open up because his ball will get far downfield faster than mine. Hence, the Steelers have always preferred to stretch out a defense and allow their receivers to come into the open for bigger gains. Yet, I'll bet that if I examined his playbook, I would find that he uses the same basic pass patterns that we do in Cincinnati.

Our basic philosophy—and one with which I totally agree—is that we will take any completion that we can get. That makes me an easy quarterback to keep happy because I am more than willing to take a four-yard gain on first down; at second-and-six, I still have many options going my way. That means, as I noted in the preceding chapter, that if the first receiver in my progression list comes open four yards past the line of scrimmage, I'll not look him off and wait for the second or third guy to be open for a bigger gain, because I want that sure yardage.

I know that there is a tendency for many young quarterbacks to say, "Ah, there's a guy open short but I'd like to get another receiver open a little deeper." So they wait to get the deeper receiver, and what often happens is that the deep receiver really doesn't come open, and when the quarterback looks back to the first one, he's been covered, too. So now that quarterback has lost his options. The message here is that a quarterback should be patient in his thinking and not get greedy. He should take what is there because that first receiver is open for a very definite reason and the odds are that he will connect with him many more times than he will waiting for that deep throw to be open. I'm not saying that this rule applies right across the board. Obviously, if it is third-and-twelve, I want to throw the ball beyond twelve yards and get the first down. At the same time, if that twelve-yard receiver is covered, I am not going to try to force the ball to him and risk an interception. That means I will go down my progression list, and if my only receiver can get just five or six yards, I'll throw him the ball. That's six yards extra on my team's punt. Then let the defense come on and play. Football is a team game, and the special teams and defense are part of it, too. The worst approach that a quarterback can take is to believe that he has to do it all himself on offense.

Of course, there also is an exception to that rule. Obviously, if it is late in the game and a team needs a lot of points to try to catch up, that third-and-twelve pass may have to be pushed into a crowd and a hoped-for reception (or possible pass-interference call), because the team needs the ball and all of the plays that it can make. But if the team is in the ball game, a quarterback shouldn't take it out by making foolish mistakes, most of which result in some cheap and easy points for the opposition. Just remember how many times those so-called six-yard throwaways have turned into big gainers. All it takes most of the time is one missed tackle, and the receiver can be off and running.

There also is one other strong belief that I feel will apply as we begin our discussion of the various types of passes and when to throw them, and that concerns the ball's path. My particular preference is to throw many of my passes low and allow my receivers to go to the ground to make the catch. Obviously, if a receiver is wide open I will get him the ball where he can easily catch it and keep going, but the key there, as in throwing it low, is to find a safe spot to place the ball.

I have always equated it with how Jack Nicklaus plays golf. If he is hitting to the green and he knows there is a bunker or rough on the left, he still will aim for the green but he will take a little extra care to see that, should he miss, it will be to the right, in an area that he can easily chip from, not to the left where there is so much trouble. That's like throwing a pass. If I am not going to complete it, or if I feel there is going to be a problem completing it, I will aim the ball low, or away from the defender, to make sure that if my receiver can't get it, then neither will the defensive back nor linebacker.

The technique that I favor is to allow the receiver to make either a "little-fingers-together" or a "thumbs-out" catch when he has to reach down for the ball. The "little-fingers-together" forms a perfect bowl for the ball to land in, and all the receiver need do then is to grasp it; the "thumbs-out" technique opens both hands, and he again has a nice target in which the ball can land, and then be grasped. Conversely, when a receiver has to stretch for a ball with his thumbs in, it forces him to extend his body a great deal, and receivers simply don't like to offer such inviting targets to the defense. When I throw a ball below a receiver's waist, I try to allow him to make a thumbs-out catch, because he can adjust quicker if the ball is at his belt or a little bit lower. That helps me to throw the ball with more accuracy into tighter holes and also get it to the receiver quicker off his break, because I can put the ball in a position where he can catch it immediately, and not have to move or stretch too far. This helps a quarterback because he will be aware of the safe areas in which to throw the ball, the ball's destination; and if he takes care to see that it doesn't fall into the wrong hands, he will be avoiding a needless number of interceptions.

When we outlined the three basic pass drops—three, five and seven steps—in the last chapter, we touched on what passes can best be thrown from each position. It is important to coordinate the pattern run with the drop position because the quarterback cannot sit back waiting for receivers to break into the open, and he cannot have the receiver making a break when he is not ready to throw. For instance, if the receiver is running a ten-yard pattern and the quarterback is taking a seven-step drop, the receiver obviously will be breaking into the open before the quarterback is ready to throw, and that just destroys the pattern's timing. By the same token, if the receiver is running a sixteen- or seventeen-yard pattern and the quarterback takes a three-step drop, he obviously is ready to throw the ball before the receiver is even thinking about making his break.

To repeat: the three-step drop is for very quick patterns, the quick outs and the hitches, the little slants or a quick look-in pass to the tight end; the five-step drop is ideal for ten- and twelve-yard patterns, such as the tight end over the middle (we give our tight ends flexibility in running a lot of different option pass routes, all geared to the kind of coverage they are seeing); and we'll use the seven-step drop if we are trying to get a receiver on a deep crossing pattern, a deep comeback pass, or what we call a "shake," where the receiver runs toward the goalpost and then cuts his route toward the corner.

Using the "passing tree" diagram as a reference, we will discuss each pattern, starting with the short ones which are used with the three-step drop:

1. Quick Out: The receiver will run about five yards and then break to the outside, while the quarterback will take a three-step drop. The ball must be thrown out in front of the receiver toward the sideline so that, at best, he can make the catch and, at worst, it will land out of bounds or he will catch it and go out of bounds. Too many times every season a quarterback will throw this pass without really facing his target, and the ball will sail behind the receiver—or in the direction of the pass defender, and the defender will be off to the end zone with the interception. But that mistake will not happen if the ball is thrown low and away, because that in itself forces the receiver to come back toward the ball, and if he must go down for it, the defensive back cannot get to it.

For the "quick-out" pattern, the quarterback takes a three-step drop and the receiver will break toward the sideline after running five yards (photos 4-1, 4-2). The ball must be delivered as the receiver makes his break and put low in front of him so he will come back to catch it (photos 4-3, 4-4, 4-5).

4-1

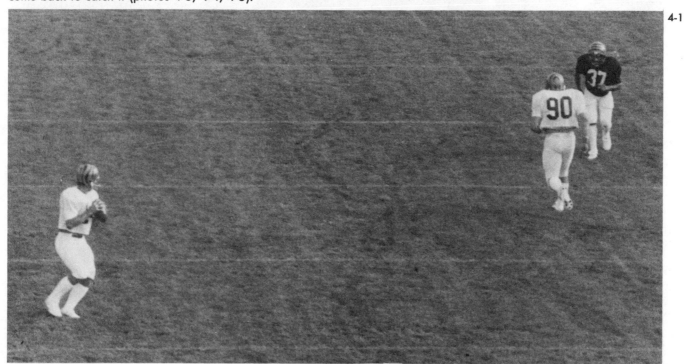

4-2

4-3

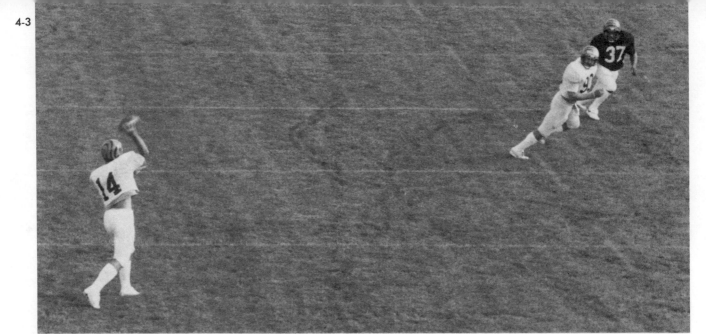

4-4

4-5

2. Hitch: This is related to the quick out, the difference being that the latter will break toward the sideline while the hitch goes five yards with the receiver stopping to face the quarterback. Both passes are good first-down plays, or if a quarterback sees a cornerback playing pretty loose, he can get a quick five or six yards with a quick audible to this type of pass, and that is generally when it is used. Of course, with a quick receiver like Cris Collinsworth, John Jefferson or Wes Chandler, this kind of play can suddenly become very big with one missed tackle.

The "hitch" pattern is the reverse of the quick out because the receiver runs his five-yard pattern and turns toward the center of the field (photos 4-6, 4-7). The quarterback must anticipate the move and throw the pass as the receiver hits his break point (photo 4-8). The receiver then moves back toward the line of scrimmage to catch the ball (photos 4-9, 4-10).

4-6

4-7

4-8

4-9

4-10

3. Slant: This pattern, with a three-step drop, is used primarily near the goal line when defenses shift into more man-for-man coverage. Twenty years or so ago, when man-for-man coverage was so prolific, this was a very big play at any part of the field for fast receivers. Norm Van Brocklin, a Hall of Fame quarterback, and Tommy McDonald used it as their specialty when the Philadelphia Eagles won the NFL title in 1960; and Bart Starr, another Hall of Famer, and Boyd Dowler of the great Green Bay teams of the sixties were deadly when they used it. All a swift receiver needs is a step on the defensive back and to have the ball delivered where he can catch it running at full speed, and the end zone will be the next stop.

In using this kind of pass, quarterbacks must think also of the physical well-being of their receivers, so very important if they are to establish a mutual confidence. Receivers know they are sitting ducks when they go cruising across the middle of a defense because their bodies are exposed to the special mayhem that defensive backs use to protect their territory. Therefore, receivers tend not to go after a ball aggressively if it is thrown high and out in front of them because they know they might get a shot to their face.

However, if the quarterback puts the ball out in front but still low enough, they won't mind going down for it because they feel safe and secure that they will not take a brutal hit head-on. Many times on first down near the goal line, a quarterback will show the linebacker a play-action move to keep him close to the line of scrimmage, then throw the slant behind him. But it is not effective in the middle of the field against zone defenses because the receiver will be cruising through inhabited areas.

The "slant" pattern is effective against man-for-man coverage and is thrown off a three-step drop (photos 4-11, 4-12). The quarterback will throw the ball as the receiver makes his cut (photo 4-13) and far enough out in front so the receiver will get it at full stride (photo 4-14) and low enough so he can catch it without extending his body (photo 4-15).

4-11

4. Square Out: This is a ten- or twelve-yard pass, depending upon a team's particular offensive philosophy, thrown very nicely off a five-step drop. The ball must be thrown before the receiver breaks because it is in the air longer than a quick-out pattern. That means the defensive back has more time to recover and go after it, so the receiver must be driving him backward while the ball is coming. He then will break and catch the ball as the defender tries to jam on the brakes and come up to make the play. If the ball is thrown out in front of the receiver and low, it is a very safe pass. Our guys get a lot of dirty knees with this kind of pattern, but they also get a lot of catches. This also requires many hours of work between quarterback and receiver because of the intricate timing that is necessary when throwing the ball. Both quarterback and receiver must know where the ball is going and when it is going to arrive. This close work also cuts down the chances of misfiring and forcing an interception.

The "square out" is a ten- to twelve-yard pass thrown off a five-step drop (photos 4-16, 4-17) and before the receiver has broken toward the sidelines (photos 4-18, 4-19). The receiver must come back to catch the ball, which must be thrown low and in front of him (photos 4-20, 4-21).

4-16

4-17

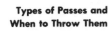

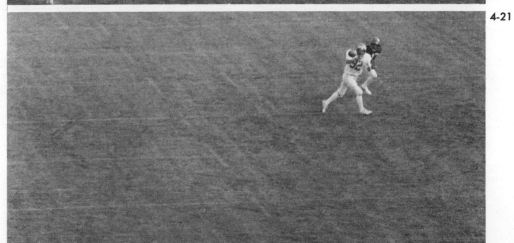

5. Crossing Pattern: Depending upon a team's philosophy, this is between fifteen and twenty yards to a receiver who will run straight down the sideline and then break across the middle; it is usually thrown from a seven-step drop. How the ball is thrown depends upon the coverage: in man-for-man, the ball should lead the receiver away from the defender; if the defense is using zone coverage, the quarterback should concentrate on throwing the ball quickly when the receiver makes his break.

Remembering that receivers do not feel comfortable going across the middle to catch the ball, I try to aim it low if they are going to be in a tight spot so they can go down on their knees to catch it, and not get hit in the face by the free safety. None of us will ever forget the shot that Pat McInally, one of our wide receivers, took from defensive back Thom Darden of the Browns during a game at Riverfront Stadium in 1980. Pat caught the ball with his body partially extended, and Darden hit him high. He was carried off the field on a stretcher, and many of us feared that he was seriously injured, but happily that tough Irishman fooled us all. He came back and played in the fourth quarter and even caught a touchdown pass.

There are also times when running a crossing pattern that the quarterback will have to "feather" or put some "touch" on his throw. For instance, when a linebacker is ten yards away and the receiver is open twenty yards away, the quarterback obviously cannot wait to throw it between the linebackers, so he must arch his throw or "feather" it over the linebacker's head. This means throwing at a slower velocity, but with enough "touch" that the linebacker cannot reach or jump to intercept it. If a quarterback miscalculates a linebacker's jumping ability, the ball may go directly into his hands. Linebackers are not as agile as receivers in going after a pass that is thrown low, so they have a harder time going across a receiver to knock it down or to intercept it, which is one very good reason to throw it low.

It also is important not to try to do too much feathering in tight situations, because the ball's slower velocity gives the safety an opportunity to adjust his position and target the receiver for a hard shot. If I can't throw the ball between linebackers and throw it low and hard, then I tend to junk that pattern and go to another receiver on my progression list, because I don't want my receivers to get hit that much. You'll often see our receivers go down to the ground when they go across the middle in tight coverage because they know I will throw the ball at that level. Of course, if there is no free safety, then the quarterback will have the perfect opportunity to allow his receiver to catch the ball on the run.

Using a seven-step drop, the quarterback throws a "crossing pattern" to a receiver who has run fifteen to twenty yards down the sideline and then breaks to the center of the field (photos 4-22, 4-23). If he is facing man-for-man coverage, the quarterback's pass should lead the receiver away from the defender (photos 4-24, 4-25, 4-26) and it should be aimed low so as not to force the receiver to extend and expose his body (photos 4-27, 4-28). In zone coverage, the quarterback must throw the ball quickly when the receiver makes his break.

4-22

4-23

4-24

4-25

4-26

4-27

4-28

109

An offshoot of this pattern is something we call the *post corner*, or *shake*, where the receiver will break across the middle and then head for the corner. This is a prime example of where a passer will have to put some "touch" on the ball, or even slow down the receiver in the zone to allow him to catch it. Often this pattern will be used to split the zone coverage, and the receiver will have one cornerback in front of him and the safety behind him. The passer then tries to put the ball in the area between the two defenders, aiming it low so that either it will hit the ground for an incompletion or the receiver will have an opportunity to go down for it and not take a ferocious hit. The receivers don't mind going toward the sidelines for the ball because they are not going to get hit head-on.

Putting a "touch" on the ball was one of the most difficult things I had to learn when I came into pro football, and later in the book we will outline a good drill for young quarterbacks that will help them become more adept at it.

The other move—slowing down the receiver—means that if the quarterback finds his receiver open in the zone defense on any pattern, he doesn't want him to continue to an area that may be patrolled by a linebacker or defensive back. So he should throw the ball at him, rather than trying to lead him. This will slow down the receiver's pass route and force him to come back for the ball. Collinsworth and I work this well together because Cris can adjust to the ball so well.

In the "post corner" or "shake" pattern, the receiver will start out with a crossing pattern move (photos 4-29, 4-30, 4-31)

4-29

4-30

4-31

and then cut his route back toward the sideline (photos 4-32, 4-33). As soon as the receiver cuts toward the sideline, the quarterback will throw (photos 4-34, 4-35) and either allow him to run under the ball or, in tight zone coverage, slow him down by forcing him to come back and catch the ball (photos 4-36, 4-37).

4-32

4-33

4-36

4-37

4-34

4-35

113

6. Post Pattern: So called because the receiver runs on an angle toward the goalpost. I won't throw this pass if there is a free safety, while Dan Fouts of the Chargers will throw it very quickly—off a five-step drop—and so often he'll beat the free safety by getting the ball to a receiver before the defender can move to cover. Some offenses will put in the post pattern as an automatic call whenever there are certain types of blitzes, using a three- or five-step drop, because there will be no free safety in those types of coverages. That often puts a receiver in man-for-man coverage, and a receiver with great speed can beat a single defender and, if the quarterback survives the blitz, make a big play.

The key to success is putting the ball in front of the receiver so that he must run to catch it—hopefully in full stride—thus pulling him away from the defensive back. The ball should not be thrown on a straight line up the field because the defensive back will have a chance to make a play on the ball, but it should go at an angle with the route the receiver is taking toward the goalpost.

7. Comeback: The receiver may run eighteen to twenty yards along the sidelines, then stop and come back toward the line of scrimmage. It is important that he make that move backward because he will have a defensive back on his inside, and the ball, at that distance, will be in the air quite awhile. So if he comes back to catch it, he will be running away from the defensive back and he can use his body to protect the ball while making the catch.

To me, throwing low is the safest bet because the receiver must keep his

4-38

The "hook" pass sends a receiver about sixteen yards downfield (photos 4-38, 4-39, 4-40) where he rolls into the open areas between the linebackers.

feet in bounds, and it sometimes is a bit easier to do this by going down to catch the ball. It means that he also won't have to concentrate on reaching for the ball, worrying about his feet and wondering where the defensive back is going to hit him. Of course, if the defensive back falls down or lays well back, the receiver can catch the ball and then turn and perhaps make more yardage, rather than simply stepping out of bounds.

Another pass in this same family, and which should be thrown the same way, is the *deep square-out* pattern, perhaps the toughest of all passes to throw because the ball must travel the farthest distance in a short period of time, and still be timed to hit the receiver near the sideline. Normally, these are fifteen- to twenty-yard patterns where the receiver will start downfield and then break to the sideline. Ball and receiver must come together simultaneously, which means the quarterback has to throw the ball even before the receiver makes his break. The stronger a quarterback's arm, the later he can wait to throw the ball, and conversely the weaker the arm, the longer it takes the ball to get there, so it must be thrown earlier. Bradshaw is a good example of a quarterback who could wait till the last instant and then throw to a spot that nobody else can reach. Bert Jones, before he injured his arm, was the same way. They could get the ball in places that I never would consider.

8. Hook: This is a first cousin to the comeback pass, the difference being that the receiver will go down the field about sixteen yards and then try to hook between the linebackers in the zone. It is important to put the ball in an area where the receiver can use his body to protect it from the defensive

4-39

4-40

4-41

The quarterback must throw the ball before the receiver makes his cut and put it where he can protect it from the defender (photos 4-41 through 4-45). An offshoot of this pass is the "comeback," where the receiver runs along the sideline for sixteen to twenty yards, stops and comes back toward the line of scrimmage. The ball is thrown the same way.

4-44

4-45

4-42   4-43

back, who really has to come through the receiver to make a play on the ball. A lot of pass interference calls come on this play because the defender often mistimes his coverage and moves into the receiver before he has the ball. This is another pass that I'll aim low to reduce some of the punishment my receivers will receive from the defense.

9. Streak: Some teams call it a "Go," or the quarterback may say in the huddle, "Run as fast as you can and I'll throw it as far as I can." But how far the ball is thrown is not as important as the technique in throwing it. I throw it high to "get some air under it," and I try to keep the ball to the outside so the receiver can run under it as he fades away toward the sideline. This gives him an opportunity to use his body to protect the ball. We get nearly as many interference calls on this play as we do completions.

The "streak" or "go" pattern can be thrown from a five- or seven-step drop, depending upon a quarterback's arm strength and the receiver's speed. I may let the receiver get a jump (photos 4-46, 4-47, 4-48) and then throw the ball high and to the outside of the field so it will come in over his outside shoulder as he fades away toward the sideline (4-49, 4-50), allowing him to use his body to protect the ball. Caution: Don't throw this pass when the cornerbacks are playing deep.

4-46

4-47

When I am going to throw this pass to Isaac Curtis, I'll take only a five-step drop and throw it as far as I can, hoping that he won't outrun it and have to stop to make the catch, giving the defensive back time to get back into the play. Bradshaw and Steve Bartkowski of Atlanta, who can throw a ball seventy to eighty yards, can wait a bit longer and work from a seven-step drop because the ball is going to travel farther and a lot faster.

Speed is not an absolute prerequisite, though. When Chip Myers played wide receiver for the Bengals in the seventies, he had only average speed, and the defenses never believed that he could go after a pass like that. Consequently, he was ignored quite a bit and managed to get open deep very often and made some big plays. Chip would always get on me if I first looked to Isaac instead of him, because he started to believe that his "speed" was getting it done for him.

When we played the Houston Oilers in the final game of the 1982 season, we played a little game with the streak pattern. On one play, we put Collinsworth inside Curtis and let Cris catch a quick slant. We thought we could fool their cornerback and run the same formation again, only change the play to a streak to Isaac. I faked to Cris on the slant, then hit Ike on a 44-yard touchdown play on which he made a tremendous over-the-head catch that also kept alive my record-setting completion streak of twenty straight passes. In that situation, the use of the streak turned out to be more of a finesse play because we lured the cornerback inside to cover Collinsworth and went behind him with the streak.

That also points up when *not* to throw that pattern—when the cornerbacks are playing deep. The receiver never will catch up to him, and in the end, there will only be a jumping contest for the ball. So don't throw it into their coverage, but come back instead to an alternative receiver. A quarterback must make sure that he has the right situation to make this play successful—if the defensive backs are crowding the line of scrimmage, or if we believe our receiver can run past the defensive back.

We throw so many ten- and fifteen-yard routes that the defenses sometimes tend to squat right down on us; their defensive backs plant their feet at those ranges waiting for our receivers to make their breaks and for the ball to be delivered. Those are the times when we can get a move around a defender and throw the streak. But when teams such as Tampa Bay, Houston and San Diego, which play a lot of zone defense, will not let your receivers get behind them, then we must settle for the shorter routes before we can even think about going long.

This brings me to one very basic philosophy that I will repeat several times: *Do not force a play that is not there.*

10. Swing Pass: We will now discuss running-back passes. Our version of the swing pass usually will send a back toward the sideline after he makes a bit of a swing, or "belly," and then straightens his route so that he will be able to catch the ball at full stride going toward the line of scrimmage. When the defense is backing up and he is going at full steam as he makes the catch, it is a great way to get the ball outside and allow a very quick back to get into the open where he can use his running instincts, power, speed and moves.

As simple as the swing pass may look, it, more than any other throw, demands greater emphasis on the quarterback throwing the perfect pass. The quarterback must deliver the ball so that the back will not have to break stride by stopping for it, reaching behind to catch it or having to leap for it. Running backs simply are not as adept as receivers at making adjustments in catching errant throws, so if a running back gets a poorly thrown pass, chances are that he may not make the catch simply because he isn't able to make the quick body adjustments. The quarterback can also improve the chances of a completion by taking a little something off the ball's velocity, because the running back will be at relatively close range. Sometimes a ball thrown too hard will bounce off a back's hands and chest and into the air where it becomes a choice plum to be plucked by an eager linebacker. There never is any need to gun a ball at a running back, though the quarterback doesn't want to soft-lob it either. The timing of the throw is the key ingredient in giving a back peace of mind and allowing him to see the ball into his hands. A late throw often allows a linebacker to get into the play, and backs get skittish when they see potential tacklers making a move toward them. That can destroy their concentration in making the catch.

The swing pass often is used as an outlet throw when all the other possibilities for getting a receiver downfield don't work out; therefore many times the quarterback will be throwing the ball in the last fraction of a second before the defense closes in. He still must take as much care with the throw under these conditions as he does when utilizing the back as a primary receiver. Therefore, both the running back and the quarterback must work diligently in practice during the week to perfect their timing.

Throwing in the face of a pass rush requires the utmost cool, and often under these conditions a quarterback will make an error, either by trying to force the ball into an area where there is tight coverage or by throwing a bad pass. Both are apt to be picked off, and while the quarterback might try to console himself with the fact that he was "only trying to save being sacked," some very serious damage can result. When the quarterback goes back to pass, the defensive line, and any linebackers who rush, have only one thought: get the passer; and even if they don't, they certainly want to rattle him enough so that he makes a mistake or becomes jumpy and loses his effectiveness.

I'm sure there is a look of terror in the eyes of every quarterback who sees these big guys barreling down on him, but you know, sometimes that look, if play-acted properly, also can lead to the success of a play that can go a long way in negating a torrid pass rush: the *screen pass*.

11. Screen Pass: This is the airborne version of the draw play, a maneuver designed to lure the defense into the quarterback's lair in the expectation of sacking him, only to see him suddenly unload the ball to an offensive player who will have a convoy of blockers. For the quarterback, the play's success requires a combination of patience, courage and more than a little acting ability.

There are several types of screen pass, the most common being the *slow screen*, which really is built on a three-second count before the ball is thrown. There also is a *read screen*, where the quarterback will first look to

121

throw to a receiver down the field, and if he is covered, then goes to a running back who may have one or two blockers in front of him. We have seen in recent years the evolution of *tight end* and *flanker screens,* where either man will take a step or two downfield, then come back and get a quick pass as a convoy of linemen sweep out to form a protective wall. We'll discuss each in turn.

The "slow screen," the granddaddy of them all, is timed by all of its participants, who are mentally counting, "A thousand one . . . a thousand two . . . a thousand three . . ." by which time the ball should be thrown to a back, who then yells, "Go," to his linemen and they all begin to move downfield. The timing and final signal are important because the linemen can move across the line of scrimmage when the ball is thrown but they cannot block anyone until it is touched by the receiver.

The running-back receiver will usually set up as if to block, and once he sees the offensive linemen "release" the pass rushers, he will move to a spot behind them so he can be in a position to catch the ball.

The linemen have to be actors, too, and look as if they are trying to fight off the rushers. All of this takes only a moment, perhaps after the rusher's first move into the blocker. Once a pass rusher feels he is beating the blocker, then he thinks only of getting to the quarterback. As soon as the rushers are gone, the offensive linemen immediately begin to form their screen—right, left or middle—and they are joined by the running back.

For the quarterback, there comes two or three seconds of terror sometimes, because he must attract those defensive people to him, first by looking downfield as if he is searching for a receiver, and then by slowly drifting back and bringing them away from the budding screen. If he doesn't "sell" the screen, then those defensive guys will smell the deception and immediately fan out to take away the play. Then the passer is in trouble, because there won't be much room to run and too little time to look for another receiver. Oddly enough, the play also can be spoiled by a slow pass-rushing lineman who may wind up in the midst of the screen because he was not aggressive in going after the passer. Here, the offensive linemen have the responsibility of policing the area and knocking the guy down, if necessary. Often a defense does this by design, designating the lineman as a "traffic cop," left to guard the middle against draws and screens.

The quarterback's final act is to get the ball to his receiver, and sometimes this is the toughest of all. There are no hard-and-fast rules, just get him the ball. This means being creative sometimes if I can't dunk it over the onrushing linemen. I've even seen quarterbacks throw the ball underhand to get the play going. The onrushing linemen are the people whom the quarterback must beat. Sometimes it means dropping back farther to get a passing lane, or throwing it higher over their heads, or whatever it takes.

The quarterback also must keep sight of his receiver, who sometimes will get caught up in all of the traffic or get knocked down and thus leave the play naked. Here is the perfect example of where a passer can make a bad play worse if he tries to guess where the receiver will be. If the back is covered, throw the ball on the ground at his feet and avoid taking a loss; if there is no one to receive the ball, the passer usually doesn't have time to throw it away, with the pass rush so close, so he just must eat it and take the loss.

Forcing the ball with no idea of where it will land is only inviting disaster. There is no doubt that these are scary moments while this ruse takes shape because the passer really is at the mercy of that rush until he gets rid of the ball safely and accurately. During our down years in the late seventies, I developed some bad habits with this play because I was getting sacked so much that it became almost second nature to try to unload the ball early. After our protection picked up and I was getting more time to throw on all patterns, I caught myself still rushing the screen pass, so I had to get back into the rhythm and regain some patience. Under any conditions, it is hard to be patient in a pass rush, but this is another form of the special discipline and poise that a quarterback must have to be successful in all situations. The reward comes after that back catches the ball and those big offensive linemen begin to mow down the linebackers and defensive backs. Even on the field, I can feel the stadium come alive when the fans sense that we have something really good on the move.

Dan Fouts, in San Diego, and my good friend Jim Hart, in Washington, are two of the best at executing the "read screen." They go through their progression chart of receivers, and while doing that a lineman will come out to be ready to convoy a back if he is to be used as the final outlet receiver. Of course, if a receiver is open downfield, then the screen part of the play will be forgotten.

The other kinds of screens are quick-starting plays. There is one where a quarterback can quickly look downfield for a receiver, then go right to a running back on a count of "a thousand one . . . a thousand . . . throw." The back will get a quick screen of blockers, and the quarterback will toss him a little flare pass. Of course, like the read screen, the passer has the option of going to that receiver downfield if he is open; but he cannot wait too long nor worry about play-acting as much because the play's effectiveness is designed for its quick starting.

Space also is essential when using the receiver screens. So is the necessity for having receivers who can run as well as a running back after they catch the ball. Good examples are James Lofton of Green Bay, Wes Chandler of San Diego, and our own Isaac Curtis and Cris Collinsworth. Normally, the play will begin with a play-action fake to allow the receiver to start down the field and then retreat, and also to keep the defense looking inside for a possible run. At the same time, one or two linemen will get to the area, or possibly a back or another receiver will go in motion to that side to form the blocking screen. I try to pass the ball to a point where the receiver, after having made his move backward, will have to reach for it. This gets him going forward again, and he then can get in behind his screen.

This is not as easy as it sounds because there are several dangers to which the quarterback must pay heed. First is to be sure that the throw goes forward. If the receiver comes back behind the quarterback and the ball is thrown on that plane, then it is a lateral and a free ball if muffed; or if it goes out of bounds, then that is the spot where the ball will be marked for the next play and an obvious loss.

If the defense is playing bump-and-run, no one will be fooled because the defender will come up quickly to play the receiver, so the best thing the quarterback can do is to throw the ball away—throwing in a forward di-

123

rection, of course. This is another instance where, if a quarterback is not careful, he can make a bad play even worse by trying to force the ball. Defensive backs love these situations because it gives them a chance to intercept and run for an easy score.

When the quarterback uses any of the passes we have discussed, he wants the six points going *his* way.

Chapter 5
Mental Preparation

TAKING into account that a quarterback must have a good passing arm and adequate athletic skills, his job then really requires more mental work than it does physical labor. He must be able to think under the most adverse pressure situations and also be able to function competently when the defense is doing everything possible to make him uncomfortable with his game. He must be able to utilize his own talents yet not try to exceed his own physical ability.

He must be what I call "a smart quarterback" because it means understanding the receivers he can rely on in tight situations . . . when a key offensive performer is a little tired and not functioning at full capacity . . . knowing when to work his best running back again and again . . . knowing who on defense is vulnerable to a pass which he will call in a key situation . . . or recognizing when a key defensive player may be tired and a step or two slower. He must be capable of knowing and recognizing all of this and yet be able to make the parts of his team function within twenty-five to thirty seconds of seeing the ball marked ready for play, or within three seconds after taking the center's snap and looking for an open pass receiver through a maze of defenders' arms and bodies.

If he must think about what he wants to do in these split-second situations, then it will be too late to do anything worthwhile. Yet, if he has worked at preparing for a game, long before he ever reaches these critical situations, enough time and effort have gone into the thinking process so that it really gives way to reacting to the situation and doing what is necessary to succeed. If a quarterback does not understand the importance of the mental part of his job, then he simply will not be successful at any level, never mind trying to make a living in professional football.

My first NFL coach, Paul Brown, always called this kind of pressurized decision making the true artistry of being a coach—and, I must add, in relation to the quarterback, it really separates the artists from the run-of-the-mill guys. It means the ability to do the right thing at the right time at the right place most of the time under the stress of a game. Coach Brown always told us that poise under stress is the key to maintaining a consistent and winning level of play, and that in turn is linked to the capacity to learn. Players, especially quarterbacks, who don't have it are invariably the first to make the big mistakes in a close game because they cannot handle the pressure.

Thus the importance of paying so much attention to the mental side of the game, and that begins with the first day of preparation when the coaching staff begins to discuss the *scouting report* on the upcoming opponent. This is nothing more than a breakdown of that team's playing talent and what it does best—and not so good—under different situations and from different areas during a game. For instance, we will learn under what conditions a team will insert its nickel defensive back. On some teams he may come in on any down when the offense needs seven or more yards for a first down; others may insert their nickel back when a team needs eight or more yards; still others may do so when a team needs five or more yards, but only on third down.

Our reports will tell us which defensive backs can cover well man-for-man and which are vulnerable. Thus, we always will be looking to force the matchups that will suit our offense, getting Isaac Curtis or Cris Collinsworth in man-for-man situations with the backs who cannot cover. They tell us which pass rushers are the most aggressive and whether they may be vulnerable to traps and screens, and which ones are slower, so that we may want to move our pocket a bit toward a certain person and relieve some pressure on passing situations. They will tell us the physical skills of the linebackers, and who reacts best against the running game, or which ones drop back and react quickest in passing situations. Of course, the report will tell us, too, who is the most vulnerable in these areas.

Scouting reports also will tell us the defensive tendencies of our opponents from every spot on the field, depending on down and how much distance is needed for a first down. Our defensive team is also receiving the same kind of report about our opponent's offense; and the opposition, of course, is hearing a complete breakdown of all that we do, and how well our team does it, player-by-player, unit-by-unit.

These written reports, which are culled from hours of watching our opponent's films and from the report of a scout who has watched that team in person, also will detail the individual matchups we will face, with the player's height, weight and speed for the forty-yard dash. If a player has been injured recently or slowed by any physical mishap, it will note that, as well. It will tell us if a player has been having problems of late handling a specific kind of play or move, or if he has changed his style from the last time that we played against him. It will note if that change is for the better or for the worse, and suggest ways of better dealing with his method of playing.

In short, this report would be the envy of the CIA in its most sophisticated intelligence operation, because there will be very little about the opposing team, and all of its players, that we won't learn. I have always kept a little notebook on many of the players whom I face each year to see if there are any startling changes from year to year, and when I go to the film study part of my preparation, I use this information to see where my advantage may come.

Our offensive players are all concerned with the individuals whom they will face—the linemen versus the front three or four and the linebackers, the backs against the linebackers, and our receivers against the defensive backs. All of them study film and during the week they will come to me and say, "If we run such-and-such play, I can beat him on this move, or on that move." Although I'll catalogue these suggestions, I still must take a broader overview during my preparation. For example, if I see a linebacker lined up outside the tight end a little bit, that tips me that the defense may be set to go to a weak side zone or come with a blitz. If the free safety has his feet in a certain position, he most likely will stay back in his position and go to the ball. If they are in another position, it tips me that his rotation, or movement, will be in a certain direction.

Of course, while studying the scouting report and then adding my own film study, if a glaring individual weakness pops up, such as a cornerback with a lack of speed, then I know I will be picking on him. Or if there is a linebacker who we don't think can cover as well as the others, we will try to get our backs into a pass pattern that will take them against that lesser-endowed linebacker. Many times people have asked me, "How come you didn't send so-and-so deep against whosis? He couldn't cover my grandmother." Well, I probably did pick on that guy, but in running a game, I can't stare at one guy all the time. I must see more of the total picture of what the defense does and plan my game to take advantage of every weakness that the opposition presents us.

The scouting report is accompanied by a computer printout showing all of a defense's tendencies, and by putting the two together, we get a total picture of what we can anticipate in our next game. Add the film study to that, and there really is little excuse to go into a game ill-prepared or not be ready to play and take advantage of all that comes our way. The age of computers, particularly, has changed the manner in which we prepare because there is so much information available at a moment's notice. In the past, coaches laboriously broke down each film, charting down-distance tendencies and then tried to juggle reams of charts in planning for a game. Now they program these film breakdowns as any business will program incoming information (remember, a computer is only a keeper of information; it neither wins nor loses a game), and upon the flick of a button, all of those data are spat out in gobs of paper that tell us everything our opposition has done, from every part of the field, for the past three weeks, and even farther back if our coaches wish to add that information.

Sometimes there can be what is called "information overkill." Rather than being meaningful, this information becomes a burden that loses its effectiveness because there simply is not time to put all of it to use. There also is the *GIGO* Theory—*Garbage In, Garbage Out*, meaning that what the computer gives us is as good as what we feed it—and I cannot reiterate too strongly that computers are only an aid to success, not the reason. Man and machine must work together, and I for one am glad to have such a tool for my preparation work. I'm sure our coaches are, too, because it makes at least one former chore a bit easier.

Of course, all of this is very costly and done only in professional football and at the highest collegiate levels. There is not the capacity for such a sophisticated information-gathering process, including scouts and film exchanges, at some colleges and most high schools. This places an added burden of preparation on the quarterback to thoroughly study whatever film of an opponent that his coach can obtain, or to be most certain to thoroughly understand whatever scouting report his coach is able to draft from conversations with coaches who already have played that team. I cannot stress too strongly the need for thorough pregame mental preparation as a means for a quarterback to have the best opportunity for week-in, week-out success. We will discuss in more detail later in this chapter how best to do this—at all levels of play.

In the pros, and perhaps in rare instances at other levels, a quarterback will play against the same defensive person for several consecutive years. So he knows what he can expect, provided that he takes into account that the player probably has improved over the last time they faced each other. Still, he will know his opponent's basic tendencies and have a good idea of the player's strengths and weaknesses so that, bulwarked by the scouting report, he is able to formulate some kind of plan. That is an advantage, but everything must be weighed by what is happening at the current time. There have been instances—Pittsburgh cornerback Mel Blount is one, Houston linebacker Robert Brazile is another—where I would look out and see that same guy coming after me year-in, year-out, and I knew from the first day of practice that he would pose a threat to what I wished to accomplish.

The Steelers and the Oilers during the mid and late seventies rarely changed defensive personnel or coaches. They knew me and my players; I knew them and what they tried to do. Of course, when my personnel changed, then I knew that their coaches would formulate something a bit different to cope, but even in doing that, I always knew that good coaches, like good quarterbacks, never ask a player to do something he cannot handle. My experience against those ever-steady teams from past games dictated what I basically knew could happen against our offense on any Sunday.

The scouting report, a quarterback's own personal book on opponents, and other information sources provide the data from which the *game plan* is formulated. This is the series of plays the offense will use to counteract those down-and-distance tendencies that are noted in the scouting report. Game plans come in all sizes, types and varieties, obviously more detailed and complex in professional football than a young quarterback would see at the high school level. In fact, the farther up the ladder a quarterback goes on the competitive level, the more a game plan will change from week to week; at the major college level it will be specifically tailored for each opponent. Many high school systems make only a change or two each week for their opponents.

I know the change for me from Augustana, a Division III school, to the Bengals was startling, though my first thought when I saw my first NFL game plan was, "How nice. We don't have to put it together ourselves." In college, ours was basically two dozen plays, mostly the same each week, regardless of the opponent: Anderson sprint right, Anderson sprint left, with maybe a new wrinkle here and there. With Cincinnati, the plan was much more voluminous, as many as seventy to seventy-five plays, all detailed and specific. Of even greater impact on me was how much bigger and faster the players were who would be trying to keep us from executing that plan, and how important it was for me to adjust mentally to matching that speed and strength with my own team's speed and strength. I never had done that before, but it started me on the right foot because I had to concentrate from the very beginning on my study and application habits, and I never lost that attention.

This again underscores a point we made earlier about knowing all of the plays in the playbook—not only the duties of the quarterback but the role of every player on every play. When a quarterback goes onto the field to execute the game plan, he will find at higher levels of competition that he will be called on to help his players with their assignments; he also must understand what they must do so that he can grasp the full scope of a plan that the coaches have laid out. When he puts the scouting report, with all of the strengths and weaknesses of an opponent, against the plan that is intended to cope with those elements, he will be able to understand just what the coaches want to accomplish. If, on the other hand, he simply masters his own area, then he will go into a game without this understanding, and there is no way that a quarterback can be consistently successful if he does not understand what he is doing—and most importantly *why* he is doing it.

Young high school and college quarterbacks have said to me that they have all they can do to concentrate on the physical and mental aspects of their preparation, and still find time to pursue their studies, other outside interests, and get sufficient rest and relaxation to lead a balanced life. I fully understand those feelings, first because it happened to me that way; and second, football on those levels still is supposed to be a pastime, something that is a pleasant diversion to what is most important: education. But once a quarterback gets into professional football, he can plan on spending eight hours a day concentrating on football, and only two of those hours actually are spent on the field. The other six hours are spent in mental preparation, and even more if the quarterback is studying at home during the evening with film and the scouting reports. There is nothing else, save his family, that he really has to concentrate on, but that is why teams pay pro quarterbacks—so they won't have to worry about finding other ways of earning a living during the season.

Working with game plans is pretty much a standard routine in the pros and at most other levels of competition. The first step is always consultation with the coach. In Cincinnati, I will often get an idea of what our coach has in mind on Monday, the day after our previous game, even though the plan will not be presented until Wednesday, our first full workday for the next game. On Monday the coaches know what they want to do and as part of our postgame blowout often will run through some ideas on the field to see how feasible they might be. I generally will see the coaches again on Tuesday, our off day, when I stop by for some film and a head start on studying the various coverages used by our upcoming opponent. That means by the time the quarterbacks meet on Wednesday to receive the plan, I have a good indication of just what we will be trying to accomplish.

This Wednesday meeting is important because the quarterback can talk specifics with his coach. Coaches then assume their teaching role and tell the quarterback, with detailed explanations, exactly what they want to do, and most importantly how and why they wish to do it. It is very important at this time that the quarterback and the coach communicate to each other their feelings about what has been planned. A quarterback must tell the coach what he feels good about and what he may feel tentative about. If there is something about which he feels uncomfortable, then obviously he is not going to execute it as well as that which he feels good about. Bud Grant, the superb former coach of the Minnesota Vikings, says that the coach must become a salesman when he presents the game plan. "He must sell the efficacy of his plan to the players, and if they believe it will work, then they will find a way to make it work. If they don't believe in it, then the greatest plan in the world—in the coach's mind—is just so many Xs and Os and won't be worth very much," he says.

I have been fortunate in working with offensive coaches who have given me flexibility in such instances. They never have put me in a situation where I have to run something that I don't want to use or with which I do not feel comfortable.

There have been times when I have looked at the game plan and told a coach that I really felt good about a couple of plays, and in the game on Sunday when we have bogged down a bit, in would come word to use those plays. That has gotten some momentum going and we have snapped out of the doldrums and gone on to win. By the same token, I can understand a quarterback who feels a bit shaky about some plays, and if things aren't going well, he will be out there saying to himself, "Please don't call those plays." That doesn't do much for a guy's confidence level.

This communication process doesn't begin and end in one day, either. Throughout the week as our preparation goes forward, we evaluate what we are doing, and if I believe that something simply is not going to work and our coach sees that I have no confidence in the play, it will be tossed out. At the same time, the things that I really feel good about not only will stay put, but in a game the coach will have a tendency to stay with them longer—and sooner or later, they seem to work out fine.

Much that is in a game plan is basic, plays that we run week after week. I know the perception of some fans is that coaches draw up new sets of plays for every game, but this simply is not feasible because there just is not the time available to perfect them. We begin with our system on the first day of training camp, and under two-a-day practice conditions, we hone and polish, even though the plays are basically the same ones we have used for several seasons and with which we are most familiar. You can see how impossible it would be for us to try to perfect new sets of plays each week, and so important is this factor that last season we also drastically reduced the number of specially designed plays we would put in for each game. Though few in number each week, and particularly designed to take advantage of special situations that occurred when we played a specific team, the new plays more often than not failed to work well because we could not perfect them in just two or three practice sessions.

While we were preparing for Super Bowl XVI, many of our players, myself included, were asked if we were putting in a lot of new plays against the 49ers. There were more than a few raised eyebrows—and a lot of suspicious looks—when we said that was not possible, even for a game as important as the Super Bowl. Every team will do what it does the best—what got it to that point—and not try to muddy or muddle its offense with complex new maneuvers. I know much was made of Bill Walsh's offensive creativity for that game and the so-called new plays that he concocted, but really the 49ers did basically the same things they had done all season. And so did we.

Of course, when new wrinkles are added, the coach and the quarterback should take extra time at the blackboard to have everything clearly outlined. One of the outstanding features of the playbooks we used under Coach Brown was the first sentence under every play: Why do we want to run this play? If a player, particularly a quarterback, knows why the play is being used and is assured of its efficacy, then, as we noted, he is more apt to make it successful.

Once the quarterback is given the game plan, then he must memorize it. This is a tough mental exercise because he must remember not only the plays but also the formations that go with them, and when they are to be used most effectively. At Cincinnati, I always have received the plays by messenger guard or with our wigwagging system, so in effect I have it a bit easier than the quarterback who must call his own game. When we used the messenger guard system, all I would get was the play number; I then had to match it with the correct formation, so there were some mental gymnastics involved with that plan. Now, everything is contained in the signals I receive from the coaches on the sidelines. But regardless of which system is used, the quarterback must thoroughly know his game plan, and that will require hours of study away from the field. There are times during a practice week when my game plan is as close to me as my wife—and I often wonder whether it gets more attention in the evenings when I am home.

Every quarterback has his own system for learning the game plan, and I find it best if I can visualize all of the situations in which I will use a particular play or sequence of plays. For example, I will look at our first-down plays and set up a hypothetical situation and match it to the kind of defensive coverage that I can expect at that time. Then I will take each of my plays, say 60Y Option, and put myself at our forty-yard line, at the left hash mark and then run the play in my mind . . . the defense likes to use cover three . . . what will be my progression list from that point of the field as I look for my receivers? Then I will go through the routine again . . . defense is in cover two, and now what do I look for? What if they blitz? My scouting report says they show a 13 percent tendency to blitz on first down from that point of the field, so what will I do in that situation? From the formation that I have set in my mind, does it make any difference which receiver I might look for at once? If I use a certain formation in this situation, what adjustment can I expect from the defense? In effect, I take my entire game plan and play the opposition even before I see them on the field, based on all of the information even before I see them on the field, based on all of the information at hand. When I am confronted with the real thing on Sunday, I can react to the situation that I have faced in my mind instead of trying to figure it out on the spot.

I do the same thing with special situations or key players. Numbers, not names, are important here. All of the fans know Ronnie Lott, the 49ers' fine cornerback, by name, but I look for his number, and I know that when his defense uses cover three (we number an opponent's various pass coverages), he prefers to use an inside technique that is a bit unusual. Therefore if we are to play the 49ers, I will run the mental pictures of what he does in that coverage and how I can counter his actions. I recall our playing a team that used one nickel back in a man-for-man defense and used another for zone coverages. So when either player came into the game, I knew what he would be doing. In preparing for the game, I had visualized my pass receiver progression list against both backs in the nickel situations so that when we played them, all of my actions were automatic.

There is a good practice drill to correlate this mental preparedness by actually doing it on the field. As I visualize a pass pattern being run against our opponent's defensive alignment, I will take the appropriate pass drop, then look to where I can expect to find my first receiver; then I will turn and look to where I can expect my second to be; and then turn again to where I can visualize the third receiver. All of this is done without throwing the ball, but with the objective of coordinating my mind and body to the play and the coverage. I will do this with each pattern by visualizing the various defensive coverages so that when we actually run the play, both in practice and in the game, my movements will be precise and not suffer from wasted time searching for an open receiver. The split second I can gain with this preparation can be enough to get me a completion.

This visual preparation cannot exclude what audible calls a quarterback must make at the line of scrimmage. For instance, having gotten a running play on second down from the sidelines, I come up and find the defense stacked against the run. Do I want to stay with the call or go to a pass? If I have properly prepared myself, I already will have visualized both plays in my mind against this particular defense, so my reaction at the line of scrimmage should be instantaneous. As quarterbacks continue to progress, they soon have more respect for a 25- or 30-second time limit than the average person because they have come to discover just how little time that is to get so much accomplished; and the less they have to ponder, the smoother will be their game.

Complementing the visualization part of preparation will be loads of film watching. Every night I take home a couple of reels of film of our opponent and watch the words and numbers on my game plan come alive on the screen as I familiarize myself with their various defensive alignments. Remember, every team has the same basic formations and pass routes, so as I study film early in the practice week, I look at a defense and try to get a feel for what it did against its opponent, as well as the little things which will tip me off before the ball is snapped. As the week goes on, I then try to pit our game plan against the defense and add to that the special situations that are possible.

During an eight-hour practice day, I always start with a meeting with the coaches in which we continue our discussion of the game plan, and then look at the films of the previous day's practice. If everything is working well, we make no changes; if there are rough spots and they can be ironed out, we do it; if not, we will discard those plays altogether. Again, it comes back to staying with what I feel confident using. After the meeting, the offensive team will look at more film of our opponents so that, as a unit, we have total familiarization with what we can expect. After lunch there will be more film watching, followed by a couple of hours of work on the field, and then more blackboard and film work. I wind up leaving our practice site with more film for home study.

While perhaps only a quarter of our working day is actually spent on the field polishing our game plan, this also is a very intensive time. As I noted, we may have seventy-five plays on line for a game, but there is no way that we can practice all of them—though we will touch on our "bread-and-butter" plays a couple of times because they really are the heart of our offense and we must keep them sharpened. But most of our practice time is spent on the newer things and polishing our passing game. Because time is so scarce, there also is a premium on a player's attention span. If a player is the backup fullback, for example, he may not get a chance to run every play in practice but he must pay attention and be familiar with all of its details, because he may wind up participating in it in the game.

I know people ask, "Well, if you don't practice every play you plan on using, how can they be effective on Sunday?" The chances are that the plays that suffer the most are the special plays for that game, which, as I noted earlier, simply cannot have the polish that the basic part of our offense gets. But we get by because we are professionals and football is our business, something we think about and work on for eight hours a day, six days a week. For example, those basic pass patterns that we discussed in the last chapter all have application in one form or another in every game, so we work to polish them, perhaps altering a route to take advantage of a defensive tendency, but never tearing down the passing tree and coming up with something totally new.

All of this will be fitted and refitted as the week goes on, and everyone has input as we refine the plan. Players will come to me as they become more familiar with it and will make suggestions based on either their new knowledge or past experience against the players we will face. Perhaps Isaac Curtis will say, "After watching so-and-so on film, I think I can do this, or that, on a certain pattern." Or he may tell me what success he has had against the player in past games, and what the situations and plays were. Cris Collinsworth will talk to me about certain situations where he believes he can get deep against a back, after having studied him on film. I will remember this information so that when I am looking for a big play during the game, I will call on those players. Quarterbacks also must be careful not to feel they must use every suggestion, because there are certain guys who always claim they are open and they are always out there calling for the ball. When you look at the films, you see that there are two or three defensive guys around them, but in their mind they can make the play. Here is a situation where the quarterback must be certain of whom he can rely upon in pressure situations.

We spend part of our third practice day working on special situation plays such as short yardage, goal line, and what we will do inside the opponent's twenty-yard line. Here, we might add a wrinkle or two, perhaps some motion or a different alignment, but the caution flag always flies regarding any radical changes, because when a team gets into these situations, the last thing it needs is a breakdown caused by players not being familiar with some new wrinkles. The rule is to make the play as simple as possible, just get the offensive line firing off the ball so the linemen can knock the defensive guys backward.

Many play calls will depend on where a team is on the field. If it is a third-and-one at the thirty-yard line, the quarterback still must keep in mind that he has the option for a field goal should his short-yardage try fail, so he does not want to do anything that will take him from field-goal range. All of this requires communication with the coaches; and long before the game ever begins, the quarterback and coach should make their decisions as to what can be expected. No surprises, please, is the best rule to avoid disaster.

Against teams with good goal-line defenses, the quarterback and coach may decide to try a pass on first down for an easy touchdown. These are things that we work on in practice so that everyone will be aware of just

135

what is going to happen. The worst thing that can befall a team about to score, other than losing the ball on a fumble, is a penalty. Most times the mistakes are mental and they can be avoided by the surety an offense will get from its practice routines.

There also are special situations which will temper the preparation. How about the weather forecast? If snow is in the offing, a team will want to get as many points as it can before the playing conditions change. How about injury? Several years ago I had injured my leg and it stiffened up badly the night before the game, so I went to Bill Johnson, our head coach at the time, and told him I doubted I would be very effective that day. Snow was forecast. I loosened up before the game with some whirlpool treatments and felt I could play perhaps the first four series, or one quarter.

We went out and attacked the opposition's pass defense and jumped ahead quickly before the snow began to fall. Soon there were several inches on the ground, so Bill came to me and said, "I think we have this one in hand, so all you have to do is try to control things with the running game." As it turned out, I played the whole game, and for the last three quarters, I simply took the snap and handed off the ball as we won. That was a case of making a decision on the day of the game. If there is a key injury, the coach must decide how he will deal with that in his preparation.

Another pitfall is being too smug when a team gets a line on the opposing team's signals. That can happen, either by some inadvertent tip-off from the opposing players or by some clues that we pick up in film study. Everyone knows it and pretty soon they think the game is over—even before it has begun. I know it has happened to us, with the result being that no one did any of the basics and what was an advantage soon blew up in our faces. Certainly we will use the information in our preparation and we will look for the little tips that will help us, but the burden then is on everyone to keep working.

Finally, by Friday everything is in place, polished and ready to go, and the coaches will cut off further input. It is dangerous to try any major revisions at this time, though I have heard that Tom Landry of the Cowboys threw out a game plan and started all over again on Friday, which he later admitted can be tantamount to cutting your throat. Yet it was something that he felt had to be done. Of course, he never advocated it as a regular procedure.

We do keep our options open, and if during the course of the next couple of days I have any nagging doubts about something, we will toss it out. Our final decision really comes just before we go out onto the field to start the game when we decide what our first series of plays will be. The coaches will say, "This is what we want to start off with. What do you think about it?" If I have no objections, then we go. But if I have a different feeling, they generally will bend to my reaction.

Having laid down the basic elements that go into a week's preparation period, let's take a look at what I do from Monday through kickoff time the following Sunday to get myself ready for a game.

MONDAY: Monday is fun day—sometimes. It is fun day after a victory; it often is not so much fun after a loss, because that is the day when the coaches will critique the game films from the previous day. I always try to get to our practice facility early so I can get my prescribed weight lifting finished, and that helps to work out some of the kinks from the previous day. Getting in early also gives me an opportunity to talk to the coaches beforehand and get a good idea when my bad plays will come up in the film critique.

I don't care how long a person has been playing in the National Football League, this day can sometimes be the toughest of the whole week. Everyone is present for the films, and regardless of your status on the team, if you made a mistake, it will be there for everyone to see and to hear about. Also if you made a good play, the paeans of praise will come forth as well, but anyone who has played will tell you that it takes heaps of praise to cover the criticism for a single mistake. Many of the players will wear white T-shirts to these sessions so the sweat won't show through; others will drape towels around their neck to help sop up the perspiration, because this is a very pressurized time.

After the film session, we often go out onto the field to correct the mistakes or to get a start on our preparation for the upcoming game by running through some things that the coaches are thinking of installing, mainly to see if they are practical. We generally wind up the day's work with a whiffle ball game to break a little sweat and get as loose as we can.

This routine is a change from what teams used to do—coming in on Tuesday after having Monday off—and I like it better. For one thing, it gets guys into the training room for treatment; it wasn't unusual for a player to covet that day off so much that he would forego any treatment until returning on Tuesday. Now, the player is on the way to being healthy for the next game.

Psychologically, it is great to get the last game out of your system, particularly if the team has lost. In the past, the players would leave the stadium feeling bad about the loss, and then spend their off day worrying and fretting about what would be said in the film session on Tuesday. This didn't make for very happy days off; and even if the team won, there were mistakes, and players are such that even after a victory they eventually wind up worrying more about the mistakes they made than the fact that the team did win, so the Tuesday film session still loomed as an ordeal.

All of this having been accomplished, everyone can head for his home and relax. Most of us will watch the Monday night football game as part of our unwinding time, though I don't always see one to its conclusion because, since I have trouble sleeping on the night after a game, I am ready to fade about half time after watching the highlights of our game.

TUESDAY: Our day off, and everyone goes about his own business. If the weather is nice, I will get a golf game going with some of my teammates or friends, and I also will find time to drop by our practice facility and look at some film for about an hour or so. I want to get a head start on the upcoming preparation time and get my mind thinking about whom we will play on Sunday.

In the evening, I often take my wife out for dinner and then get to bed early. The season is so pressurized that it is necessary to take these moments of togetherness when possible, and also to get as much rest and relaxation as possible early in the week.

WEDNESDAY: The juices begin to flow for everyone, regardless of whether the team won or lost the previous week. Everything starts fresh, and if the team is doing well, the enthusiasm is starting to peak to keep up the roll; if it is having trouble, then the resolve to turn things around is just as strong.

I always get to practice early, partly because I enjoy the ambience of the locker room. It is my second home and, for me, a warm friendly place that epitomizes everything I like about football. I'm not alone in this feeling, because in talking to players who have retired, many of them say that the one thing they miss most is the camaraderie of the locker room.

I will see the coaches prior to our quarterback meeting, which generally runs from eight-thirty to nine o'clock. As I noted earlier, we discuss some of the things we will feature in our game plan so that we can begin putting them together with the overall scouting report, which the entire team will receive at the general team meeting. At the general meeting, the coaches break down the opposition's personnel as to their strengths and weaknesses. Additionally, they bring the computer printouts which show the opponent's tendencies in all offensive and defensive situations—for example, what the defense favors on second-and-six inside their thirty-yard line, or on first-and-ten at our forty-yard line—and they also touch on all of the pass coverages that we will face.

This is a tremendous information load and it is accompanied by special play sheets which our coaches have drawn up. There is room on them for us to make notes, and this is the opportunity for us to ask questions and to clear up any fuzzy points.

We will take a little break and then begin to cover the new wrinkles that will be installed for this game. This is always accompanied by some film watching to show us how the changes will take advantage of the defensive alignments, part of the process of positioning our minds to visualize what we will be doing.

After lunch, we will watch more film and then go out onto the field and begin to put all of the mental preparation into live action. In years past, teams would concentrate on their offensive plans on Wednesday, their defensive game plan on Thursday, and then review both on Friday. We don't do that, preferring to work on both every day, though we spend a little more time on the offense on Wednesday, particularly if we are installing some new plays.

After practice, we go back and look at more film, and when that session is finished, I complete my week's weight-lifting routine. I lift, not to increase my strength, but to maintain what I have built up, because during a long season there is a tendency to really wear down. My work mainly concerns my legs, with some light lifting on my upper body. Afterward, I meet with the coaches again and take home a couple of reels of film to study at night. This is the time when I begin to memorize the game plan and put it together with the film. Sometimes if I am tired—and I am not a night person who can stay up till midnight watching film and really get something from it—I will knock off my study and then get up early on Thursday morning and work for a couple of hours before going to practice. My mind is fresh then and I can better retain much of what I have seen.

THURSDAY: This begins the refinement period for the game plan. I get to practice early and then all of the quarterbacks will look at the films of the preceding day's practice to see what went good, and in what areas we may be lacking, such as perhaps missing the concept of a particular pass pattern and not getting the ball to the best receiver.

The team also will view the films of the preceding day's practice for an overall evaluation and correction, and this is followed by more blackboard and film work as a group. After lunch, there is another film session and then we go to work again on the practice field—offense and defense—for perhaps two hours. The defense gets the extra time on this day, and afterward we may watch more film before ending our day's work.

I will take home more film for study at night, normally a different game than our opponents have sent us (by NFL rules, we get the films of our opponent's three previous games, just as they get our three previous games). In addition, our coaches often make up a special reel or two of defensive coverages the opponent uses, such as what they do in nickel back situations, or a reel of all of the blitzes that we can expect. We also may have another game or two of the opponent from a previous film exchange, and I will look at that as well. I do not claim to be a film nut, but I do make an effort to look at everything that we have available on the upcoming opponent just to be sure that I have familiarized myself with all possible situations.

If we are playing a team from our division that we already have faced during the season, I will look at that film to see how they played us. Sometimes, I'll get a film from the previous year and take it home just to note any changes that the team has made in its coverages. It would be a grave mistake to content myself with the fact that, "Oh, I played this team twice last year and I know what it does."

All of this makes for busy evenings of film watching, but taken together with the game plan—which is my constant companion during these sessions—I have by now a very good idea of what we can do best against the defenses we can anticipate. I have been able to match plays and situations against defenses and, as I noted earlier, sometimes I can see something that our coaches have missed in their preparation. This is a team effort—everyone's study is important because often ideas will beget other ideas, and there is no such thing as exclusivity on something that can work to get us a victory.

FRIDAY: Our study routine is basically the same as Thursday, starting with another session of looking at film of the previous day's practice and making any needed corrections. Additionally, we will put together our short-yardage, goal-line, and two-minute offenses. This is important for the quarterbacks because in the short-yardage and goal-line situations, as well as for situations inside an opponent's twenty-yard line, the coverages will change from zone to primarily man-for-man. Scoring from inside the twenty-yard line is perhaps the most difficult of any part of the field, because the defense has less territory to cover and the requirements for precise patterns become very important.

When Paul Brown was our coach, this was primarily a brushup day, and we often spent no more than sixty to eighty minutes on the practice field. We go longer now under Sam Wyche, a normal workday, which also includes a bit more film study when the field work is completed.

And when that is finished, I am, too, because I like to relax on Friday night, perhaps take my wife out to dinner—and it will be the same place as the previous week if we had won on Sunday—and get to bed by eleven o'clock, our normal curfew for that night. Even though the players are on their own after practice, they are expected to adhere to this curfew—the same as we have in training camp and on the road—because it is the last night that any of us really gets any kind of rest. Saturday, you see, is a bit tumultuous.

SATURDAY: For the third time, we watch films of the previous day's practice to make one final check on any mistakes in our preparation. Afterward, we go out onto the practice field, without any pads, and run through some of the plays that we have installed, to be sure that everyone understands the changes.

I am not what you would call a pleasant person on Saturday. If we play at home the next day, our house generally is buzzing with friends or relatives in town for the weekend, so I will visit with them and perhaps watch some college football on television. But sometime during that afternoon, I will say, "Excuse me," and go up to the bedroom and haul out the game plan, just to make sure I have all of the situations down pat . . . what are we going to do in short-yardage and goal-line situations? . . . what will we do against the nickel defense? . . . what will we do with the ball inside their twenty-yard line? . . .

I will have dinner at home and then go to the hotel where the team stays the night before the game and seclude myself in the room for another couple of hours, again going through every play in the game plan and trying to visualize all possible situations in which we can use them. The team will have a light meal prior to curfew, often preceded by a little meeting to cover anything important that the coaches still feel needs stressing, and then it's off to bed. I don't sleep well the night before a game so I try to go to bed a little bit earlier, but invariably I will wake up a lot during the night and begin to visualize all of the situations we might encounter the next afternoon.

If we have a road game, we usually have some time from the end of practice until our chartered flight is scheduled to depart. Sometimes I will go home and change clothes before going to the airport, an easy chore since my home is close by, though if there is a time problem, I will go from the practice field directly to the plane, because I do not like to be rushed.

If the plane trip lasts several hours, I will again study the game plan. When Paul Brown was our coach, his assistants would pass out written tests about the contents of the game plan. Some felt they were given as much to help the players pass the time as to determine how much they had retained from the week's work, but still they were graded, and if someone really came up with a low mark, he would receive some fast and forceful remedial help. Coach Brown always maintained they were given to keep the players' minds on the reason for this trip, and they always had that effect.

I always felt that if a player didn't know the game plan by Saturday—for myself, if I am having trouble on Thursday, I know I am not properly preparing—then a test or special tutoring by a coach isn't going to get it done. I do know that if someone really didn't know the answer to any of the questions, he needed only to ask the guy in the next seat to help him out. This had its own benefit of getting a player to find out something he either did not know or could not remember.

If our trip is just an hour or so, I will wait until we arrive at the hotel and then go over the game plan again. The team eats supper together so there is little reason to leave the hotel, which really is all right with me, because I tend to stay close to my room where I can relax as much as possible and try to settle down for the next day's game. Our evening routine is the same on the road as it is at home—a team meeting and snack prior to bedtime, and I will try to get to bed as early as possible. But home or away, I wind up fighting for whatever sleep I can get.

SUNDAY: This is fun day. I normally will get to the room where our pre-game meal is to be served about an hour early, have a cup of coffee, glance through the Sunday papers and then spend the last half-hour with one last tour through the game plan. It is one more checklist in which I can go through everything to make sure it is firmly implanted in my mind, as well as a last chance to ask questions. After our meal, we have a short meeting and, if we are on the road, then await the bus to the stadium.

Some of our players can't stand to wait, and they will take a taxi to the stadium just to get there, have their ankles taped, and be able to relax in a football atmosphere. Not me. I get too jittery if I get to the locker room too early, and riding on the bus gets me there with just enough time to get dressed, glance at the program and read some of the feature articles, and then relax a bit before going onto the field.

At home, we are allowed to drive our cars from the hotel to the stadium, and again, I try to time my departure from the hotel to get to Riverfront Stadium about ninety minutes before the game. I always go onto the field ahead of the main group to loosen my arm so that when the team comes out for calisthenics I will be ready to throw as soon as we break into our groups. Getting onto the field also helps to dispel the butterflies. When we come back into the locker room there is just about enough time for one last get-together with the offensive coaches to decide which plays we will use to begin our first offensive series. No sooner is that finished than Coach Wyche calls us together, talks to us briefly about the game, and then leads us in a brief prayer for the safety of all players.

After that, the locker room door opens and we all file out to be greeted at home with thunderous cheers, or with sullen silence and a few boos if we are playing away from Cincinnati. By now the atmosphere is ripe with the special tension that marks every football game. It is the start of our business day, and all of our preparation, including that very studied game plan, is about to come alive.

Chapter 6
During a Game

ANYONE who has ever played quarterback knows that the pace can be hectic during a game and that there simply is no room for wasted motions, time or effort. From the time a play ends there is usually less than forty-five seconds for the quarterback either to call a play on his own or to get one from the bench and get the ball back into action.

This places a great premium on maintaining poise under pressure, which is often the single biggest lesson young quarterbacks must learn as they mature. The quarterback, as I have noted, is the leader on the field but he cannot do everything by himself; nor can he allow good plays or bad plays to alter his mental and emotional approach to the game as it proceeds. He must be able to maintain an even keel whether his team is winning or losing, not getting too carried away when it is ahead, not getting depressed and giving up when it is behind. This emotional conduct is as important as the physical skills he uses.

This all begins by getting into the pace of the game and not allowing it to disrupt the rhythm he wants to establish with his team. From the time the referee marks the ball for play, the quarterback has between twenty-five and thirty seconds to know what play he will call, take a peek at the defense to check for substitutions, step into the huddle and make his call, get to the line of scrimmage, again check the defense for alignment and special substitutions and start the play. In the National Football League, officials have stepped up the pace of the game in the past few years. As soon as the referee sees that the ball can be set for the next play, he will mark it ready and signal for the thirty-second clock to begin. The referee, at any level of play, really is like a ringmaster in a circus in the way he moves things along on the field.

A good point for quarterbacks and coaches alike to remember is that the center should set up the huddle spot as quickly as possible after the whistle has blown ending a play; and then the other players should hustle to that spot so they will be ready to receive the next play even before the quarterback steps into the huddle. Especially receivers and backs who have just run a pass play should keep this in mind. When a pass play ends, the referee will allow them to return to the line of scrimmage before marking the ball for play *unless* he sees them dawdling back to the huddle. Then it is his discretion, if the rest of the defense and offense have placed themselves on the proper side of the line, to mark the ball—even if those players are still sauntering back to their huddle. With only twenty-five or thirty seconds in which to get a play going, every second is valuable, and players who cost seven or eight seconds with their nonchalance really are hurting their team.

While the players are forming the huddle, the quarterback always is into the next play. If he calls his own game, then he probably has begun a sequence of plays and has the next one already in mind. That being the case, the quarterback will be ready as soon as he checks the down and distance, so the other players have to be ready as well.

However, with the increased use of messengers and the wigwag system, there is time between the end of one play and the beginning of the next where the quarterback must await his information. I've done it both ways. I played under the messenger-guard system during my first ten NFL seasons, and I have gotten my plays wigwagged for the past three. When I came to the Bengals in 1971, Paul Brown was using the messenger system, having introduced it to pro football with the Cleveland Browns, where it was considered revolutionary because critics claimed it went against an almost hallowed part of the game's tradition that a quarterback must call his own plays.

Coach Brown always felt his quarterback would benefit more from fresh information coming into the game from coaches who had better vantage points in press boxes than the quarterback had on the field or the head coach had on the sidelines. Coaches in those lofty heights can chart tendencies against a team's game plan and spot other keys that give some advantage to the offense, and they have up-to-date information on every play, which can make the sideline play-calling more accurate.

There may be young quarterbacks who will resent their coach sending in

Wigwagging plays from the bench has become commonplace, and each motion by the wigwagger signifies a placement within the formation. For instance, George Sefcik is telling me that the play will be I (photo 6-1), Right (photo 6-2), Tailback (photo 6-3), Power (photo 6-4), Left (photo 6-5).

6-1

6-2

the plays, or who will hear criticism by some who would belittle them as not being "smart" enough to call a game on their own, or not be a "total quarterback." I heard some of that early in my pro career when some misinformed media people still carried those erroneous notions, and I can only repeat what Coach Brown has written about that subject in his autobiography as being the best possible rebuttal:

"All this had nothing to do with questioning my quarterbacks' intelligence, nor was I ever worried about building character and initiative, two other criticisms which were tossed at us. I cared about winning games—period—and I stand on that record. We were a team, coaches and players, and if we won, that's all that mattered. If we lost, then we went down together, and I never respected any quarterback who felt the system kept him from looking like a great leader. A quarterback is an important cog in the machine, but still a cog, and I wanted to give him all the help possible. I knew no quarterback ever worked as hard preparing for a game as our coaching staff did."

The key to sending in a play, either by messenger guard or by wigwag system, is that all the coaches know what it is and what to look for; hence they can tell immediately when it succeeds or fails. If it is a trap play, the end coach can watch the tight end's block on the linebacker, the line coach can watch the guard's trap block and a coach upstairs can check the line spacing to see if it was proper for a good double-team block. The head coach then can watch the point of attack—the spot where the play will be run—and

6-3   6-4   6-5

judge its effectiveness. On a pass, the line coach watches the pass blocking to see where any breakdowns occur and why; and the backfield and receivers coaches can follow the play and judge how well the quarterback followed the progression of receivers.

All of this firsthand information allows them to judge whether that play still remains viable in the game plan. A quarterback on the field, seeing a play fail, might abandon it when only a minor adjustment might be needed to make it work. Always remember that when a quarterback hands off the ball his back is often turned halfway to the defense and his eyes are on the ball, so he cannot see how the opposition is reacting; or after he passes and is perhaps dumped or knocked backward, he also cannot get the full picture.

Coach Brown and those who succeeded him and used the messenger-guard system have always said that it was not strictly their play selection that came into the game, but rather the best possible selection from the coaches who had better vantage points than they did. They simply made the final decision on the recommendations and from what they knew to be happening; and there often were instances when they went against the recommendations and made their own choice.

Play-calling is not an instantaneous reaction but a sequence where one play will help to set up the success of the next. When we get a second-down play, the coaches already have two or three subsequent plays in their minds. Guards who shuttled these plays also got to know, according to the situation, which ones were being favored; and sometimes even before Coach Brown, or later Bill Johnson or Homer Rice, gave the word, they would call it out. All it took was a nod from the coaches to send the guard onto the field.

There have been some funny stories about how some of Paul Brown's messenger guards handled that situation, particularly since he was such a stickler for having the play run that he had called, unless the quarterback had to call an audible. And even that call had to be correct.

Otto Graham, his great quarterback with the Browns, who was in ten championship games in ten seasons and won seven of them, often got blistered unjustly by the media and fans because he was the first to work under the messenger-guard system. Otto and I were playing in a golf tournament one day early in my career and he greeted me by saying, with a laugh:

"Have you changed any plays in the huddle yet?"

I shook my head, "I'm a young quarterback and I don't want to rock the boat."

"Well, just one clue," Otto said cheerily. "When you do call an audible, make sure it works!"

A lot of those old Browns players still love to tell the story of quarterback George Ratterman, a habitual prankster, who was playing in a game when a guard arrived with a play and relayed it to him.

"I don't like that one," he snapped. "Go back and tell him I want another one."

The poor guard was stunned for a moment and actually ran a few steps from the huddle before he realized what he was doing, returned and said to Ratterman, "You go tell him yourself."

Everyone in the huddle broke up, and Coach Brown could see them laughing, but at the time he just couldn't figure out why eleven players would be laughing when a simple running play had come into the game. I'm sure the thought of someone leaving the field and going over to that great coach, who so dominated a game, and saying, "Hey, coach, that was a lousy call. How about coming up with a better play this time?" was too comical to evoke anything but laughter. Even PB laughs when he tells the story.

There were some funny moments under this system in Cincinnati, too, particularly involving my good friend John Shinners, who was one of our messenger guards and one heckuva player.

We played Pittsburgh one day and John was engaged in his usual rugged battle with Steelers defensive tackle Ernie Holmes. After one play, Shinners stepped on him after the whistle had blown, and before Holmes could see who did it, John had gone to the sideline, and Howard Fest, the other messenger, came in with a new play. Ernie didn't really care who was lined up in the guard slot; he just knew that he had been whacked after the whistle, so he just unloaded on poor Howard.

John also proved another time that it pays to get out of a game before anything bad can happen. He had botched up an assignment that helped to kill a play, so when he got back to the sideline the coaches asked, "What the hell happened?"

"It was Rufus," John said, referring to one of our tackles, Rufus Mayes.

When John came back in with the next play, he said, "Rufus, I just blamed you for screwing up that last play, but I'll square it with you after the game."

Then there was a game in Cincinnati when John came in and said to me, "Go with sixty-three," then he looked at me for a moment with panic in his eyes, and said, "Or was it seventy-three?"

"Aw, hell, call it what you want!"

Otto Graham's words came spinning back to me at that moment. Though I never was hesitant to call an audible if the situation dictated, at that moment I just couldn't think of a good reason. We ran a play and nothing ever was said, so I always assumed we did the correct thing.

But having played in the pros under both the messenger-guard and wigwag system, I prefer the latter. I found that it was a little bit more difficult getting plays with the messenger system because the linemen don't understand all the terminology, and there sometimes was confusion with the information they brought into the game. With just thirty seconds to get the ball into play, often the time factor crowded us, particularly after Coach Brown retired. He usually had the guard on the way even before the referee had marked the ball ready for play. Later, the guard having to run to the huddle, giving me the play, and then my having to take it and put it with the proper formation while giving it to the players, all caused us to fight the clock.

With the wigwag system, either the backup quarterback or a coach, both of whom are totally familiar with the system, can signal the plays and their signals give me a little more detail. To confuse the opposition's sign-stealers, both will wigwag at the same time, but only one set is correct. As we have illustrated, each signal gives a portion of the play so that, when it is finished, I have the total play just as clearly given as if someone had told it to me.

As I previously noted, the quarterback should try to check what substitutions the defense is making and also be capable of getting some on-the-spot information from his own players on the field before getting the signals for the next play. Sometimes he gets more preoccupied with this than checking

149

for the play, but if another player on the field also is assigned to read the signals, then that is a good backup system. If I miss the start of a play, he has it; if I misread the signal, he also has it and can correct me. We have the system down so that our plays come in very quickly and I still have time, before stepping into the huddle, to scan the defense for any changes.

I must add that this is another reason why every player should be fully prepared and totally familiar with every phase of the game plan. There have been times when I have not gotten the last half of the signal because the first part has me anticipating what the play will be, and I have stepped into the huddle too quickly to see a change. If another player is watching and has a full grasp of the signals, then he will catch the change. This backup system is particularly important if the phones from the press box to the bench go out of order. We had an instance in New York against the Jets a few years ago when their phones went down, and by league rule, since we were using equipment provided by the Jets, we had to take off our phones until theirs were again working. This meant wigwagging the signals from the press box to the bench, and then to me on the field. Everyone was paying attention to be sure that the signals were properly translated.

Communication to the quarterback is by no means a foolproof deal, regardless of how prepared a team is, nor can it be considered as the only way in which a quarterback can get his information. When the quarterback comes off the field, he should go directly to the head coach—even after an interception—and discuss what has happened and exchange information. The coach will tell the quarterback what his assistants in the press box are seeing, and the quarterback can tell the coach what he is seeing on the field, and he also can talk with the coaches upstairs if he desires.

The first thing I discuss in these situations is what the defense is doing and what kind of coverage we are getting. It could be that the quarterback sometimes is actually misreading some part of the coverage and that is keeping him from going to a specific receiver or to a certain area of the field. Of course, the quarterback also is anxious to hear any tips the coaches have picked up on the defense's coverage schemes which he can file away for future use.

The coaches also may note something that the quarterback is not doing, such as taking advantage of a certain coverage or alignment that can give the offense more punch. I cannot stress too many times that a quarterback is not in the game by himself, nor should he expect to bear all of the burdens of conducting the offensive part of the game. Successful quarterbacks want as much solid and useful information as they can get during a game, and one who tries to do it all on his own is heading for some disappointing game days—and can expect to wind up on the bench.

The information exchanges between quarterback and coach are especially important during the time-outs in a game when the offense is on the field. I will have my conversation and find out what the coaches want us to do, and then I like to get back to the huddle before the referee marks the ball ready for play and explain the situation to the other players. If we are in the two-minute drill, I know basically what we will do during that time so I may remind the players of our time-out situation and the need to keep hustling to the line of scrimmage after every play so we can keep things going. Or I will remind our players when to call a time-out and when to keep the clock going after a play. A new NFL rule, put into effect last season, allows any player to ask the officials for a time-out. Before, only specially designated players—Isaac Curtis and I were the only ones on our team—could do so.

There also is something to be learned during a game from talking to the players on the sidelines, though a quarterback has to know which player's information really is reliable and which ones are lobbying for their own cause. The reliability factor is so important because if the quarterback takes a receiver's word that he is getting open and then looks for him on the next play and finds that it is not true, then that is just a wasted play.

Some important tips come from the linemen, who may say to me, "Give us a little more time on this play," or they may tell me which situations are giving them trouble, or even point out a defensive player's stance that provides a clue on what he intends to do when the ball is snapped.

As I noted earlier, there also is an information exchange on the field, and again the reliability factor will be the key in what the quarterback does with it. I recall a game in Houston a couple of years ago when we had a first down near the Oilers' goal line and we failed to score on the first down. Pat McInally, our intrepid wide receiver, came into the huddle and said, "I can beat so-and-so on just a little step and get to the outside. Call it." I did and we missed. Back into the huddle he came and said, "Hey, I really can do it." So I called the play again, and this time we clicked for the score. While Pat is a great prankster and the team's resident wit, I know that he will not make any suggestions to get him the ball unless he knows they are valid, and after a guy has been in the league for nine seasons, I have to rely on what he tells me.

For some quarterbacks, there is another role during a game—that of an extra set of eyes as part of the role of being the backup quarterback. Next to the coaches, he is as important in helping me do my job as any single person on the team because he has—or should have—prepared for the game as thoroughly as I did, and while he is not on the field playing, he will be on the sidelines calling the game as it goes along.

The relationship of the starter and the backups must be very close on game day for all to succeed. The starting quarterback may have a bad day and have to be replaced by his backup. Their roles then are reversed, but their dependence upon each other never really changes.

Though I have been a starting quarterback in the NFL since my rookie season, I have also served as the backup—or "charter," which is another role for the backup—on many occasions. When I came to the Bengals, Virgil Carter was our starting quarterback, and I had a great opportunity to watch another veteran quarterback do his job. Virgil got hurt for a five-game stretch during my rookie season, and I had to play full time; and then the following season I had the job to myself, so I never had any long-term benefits of learning as the backup quarterback. For most of my career I have been the oldest quarterback on the team, and if I had a bad day, there was no one who could come to me and say, "Forget it, kid, it happened to me, too." That is my role with our young quarterbacks. On any team that has a veteran, there is an advantage for the young, relatively inexperienced quarterback in just having somebody to talk to who has been through similar experiences.

I can only go back to my rookie year when I had to play because of

151

Carter's injury. I lost all five games that I started, and that was very traumatic. We had an eleven-point lead against the Browns with four minutes to play in one of them, and Bill Nelsen brought his team back to win. On the last play of the game, I got sacked trying to pass, and the first guy on the field to pick me up, dust me off and pat me on the back was Nelsen himself.

"Hey, kid, you really played a good game," he told me.

That did a lot to pick me up, but the next week in Oakland I suffered a hip pointer and was lying on the ground in obvious pain. Ernie Wright, one of our offensive tackles, came over, picked me up by the back of my pants and said, "Rookie, get your butt back to the huddle. You're the only guy we got."

I went back and threw a touchdown pass to give us the lead, but George Blanda came on with two minutes to play in the game and took the Raiders the length of the field for the winning score—and he did it without benefit of a time-out!

The following week, we lost again at Houston, 10–6. Coach Brown called the team together after the game, and turning to me—and I'm still hurting from the previous week's hip pointer and in the depths from having lost again—he said, "Well, Anderson, this is the third game you've lost for us now." Though he always told us not to pay any heed to the things said in the emotions of a game, I was crushed as a young player to discover that the quarterback is the player who ultimately will get the blame. As I noted at the start of the book—and which was underscored for all time in my mind on that day—the quarterback gets too much blame when he loses, and too much credit when his team wins.

I obviously didn't have much of an opportunity to learn much as the backup quarterback, having to become a starter so quickly, but that was an extreme case, and it is more the rule than the exception that the backup will have time to study, observe and learn. The other side of the coin for many, including some fine young pro quarterbacks—Jack Thompson was a good example when he was with the Bengals—is getting very impatient at not being a starter after just a couple of seasons. I can understand this frustration, regardless of the level of play, but a player must understand that he does not have the experience or the knowledge to step in quickly and become a *consistently winning* quarterback . . . the key words are "consistently winning."

It also takes a unique individual to play the backup role over a long period of time, but there are rewards. Earl Morrall is a great example of a player who, after being a starting quarterback for several NFL teams, became a backup with Baltimore's and Miami's great teams. When called upon to start, he did an astounding job. He took over for Johnny Unitas in 1968 when John tore his Achilles tendon, and led the Colts to the Super Bowl and was named as the NFL's Most Valuable Player. In 1972, Bob Griese was injured and Earl started for Miami most of that season and in the first two games of the playoffs. Griese was healthy for Super Bowl VII, and Earl stepped aside as Bob quarterbacked Miami to victory over Washington, capping an unbeaten season for the Dolphins. But Morrall did so without a whimper and stayed several more seasons to finish a marvelous career. Blanda is another great example, and his heroics were so astounding in bailing out the Raiders as a "relief" quarterback that they helped him wind up in pro football's Hall of Fame.

152

My point in all of this is that the backup quarterback must continue to work as hard as the starter, with the goal not only of improving but of being ready to play when he is called on, because there will come a time when he must take over.

Yet while he is working as a backup, he must make every effort to help the starter, and above all he must not do anything that will undermine the starter. I know of times when a starting quarterback has not been going well early in the game, and on his own, the backup quarterback would begin warming behind the bench as if to signal to the coach, and the fans, that there should be a change and it should be to him. That really can upset the starter, who knows he is struggling and is out there trying to fit the pieces together. No one really knows how important it is, in those tough times, for everyone to be pulling for the guys out on the field.

What is the role of the "charter" during a game?

Besides fully preparing, as I already have noted, he must pay attention to what the defense is doing on every play, often listing each play that we run and the defense which is used for that specific down and distance. That becomes a quick reference list or chart as the game progresses. Our guys always come to me before a game and ask, "What do you want us to be aware of today?" and I will give them items to check which, in my own preparation, I see as keys to executing our game plan. For instance, Pittsburgh blitzes a lot, and many times I will not see where they come from, so they will tell me when I get to the bench. Since they know the plays being sent into the game, they also can watch the progression list of receivers and see if I am picking up people who are open on these plays. We have two backups, so one will watch the linebackers while the other watches the secondary, and if I do make a mistake, they must tell me pretty quickly just where I went wrong. There are times when the quarterback on the field may be confused and call the wrong formation, and they must pick up on that, as well. There also is a "comfort" factor in that the quarterbacks have access to all of the information being gathered during a game, and they are better able to dispense it in terms of one quarterback talking to another.

There also are cases when the starting quarterback comes out of the game and becomes the "charter," either because of an injury or because he has an off day. Both have happened to me more than once, perhaps the most memorable time being the opening game of the 1981 season against Seattle, an instance to which I referred earlier in the book. Turk Schonert went into the game trailing, 21–0, and I worked the sidelines. We went on to win, and though I was disappointed at playing poorly and having to come out of the game, I nonetheless gave my full attention to helping him.

There also are other benefits for backup quarterbacks who are thrust into a game. They can see what the opposition is doing and thus can formulate a better idea of what will be successful in the game should they have to play. One example comes to mind. Bert Jones and I were AFC Pro Bowl quarterbacks a few years ago, and while Bert was playing, I saw that the NFC really did not play by that game's specific rules concerning man-for-man pass coverage inside the twenty-yard line, and in the first quarter this cost Bert an opportunity for a touchdown.

When I went into the game in the second quarter, we got back down there again, so Charlie Joiner, who had been my teammate for four years at Cincinnati, and I put together one of our old plays to take advantage of such coverages, and it clicked for a touchdown. But that came about because I had the advantage of seeing what the defense was doing by just watching from the sidelines.

Even with all of the help that a quarterback gets during a game, he cannot escape one fact: he is an emotional human being very caught up in an emotionally played sport. How he handles this depends on his personality, and at all times he must work within its limits. Personally, I do not allow my emotions to show during a game, and I have been criticized for it. Without trying to copy anyone, I have always seen myself in the Bart Starr–Bob Griese mold, trying outwardly to keep an even keel, regardless of how the team is playing or what the score might be. Inside, I am as keyed up as any other player and no less anxious to do well.

There have been some, such as Billy Kilmer and Bert Jones, who have been tremendously emotional quarterbacks, and their fire and spirit were an asset to their teams. But they were that way off the field, as well. Whatever the quarterback's personality, he must be in charge and in control of a situation, be it good or bad, and always be consistent. If he makes a bad play, or someone else makes one, he cannot have his chin on the ground in the huddle.

As I mentioned earlier, Dave Lapham, who was one of our fine offensive guards, was quoted once as saying, "When things are going good, Ken is low-keyed. When things are going bad, he's low-keyed. I guess he is just a low-keyed guy."

I am, but I occasionally get upset during a game. Quarterbacks never should feel that, because they are the leader, they cannot show any emotions. The feelings always will be there; how they are displayed will make an impact on the other players.

Some of my teammates kid me about my "hairy eyeball," which I guess is a way I have of looking at people when they make a mental error. With that look I do not have to say a word. That is my personality, and it allows me to display my own brand of emotion. The most important point to remember is that whether a quarterback chews out people or has the "hairy eyeball," he still gets his point across to the players and they understand what he means.

In the same vein is the tendency of young or inexperienced quarterbacks to try to do too much. When a backup quarterback gets a chance to play, his first thought is to look as good as he can, when it really should be to go out and do what is best for the team. I was no different when I was young until I finally realized that there were ten other players on the field with me. A quarterback must first concentrate on controlling and guiding his players, and if he puts this foremost in his mind, then he will automatically forget about trying to make himself look good. The end result will be that everyone—the team, himself included—will look good.

The best way to cope with that problem is to remember that one play does not win or lose a game. As a team, we spend a great deal of time in training camp talking about this fact, particularly when we are dealing with our two-minute offense. The point always is stressed that the quarterback cannot try to make everything happen by himself, that he cannot force the "big play." Big plays happen of themselves, not because a quarterback leans into the huddle and says, "Okay, this is going to be a big play." I have seen quarterbacks get into a rut where they continually look for the big play, and they wind up throwing interceptions. If there is no play, the quarterback must forget it and continue to work within the confines of his offense, where hopefully there will be enough diversity that he can take advantage of the big play opportunities which *naturally* arise.

This kind of playing builds what is one of football's favorite words: momentum. This is nothing more than a continuation of almost mistake-free plays that keep the offense moving down the field. It builds confidence in all of the players and they begin to play better, to concentrate harder and soon the good things begin to happen—the "big plays."

I call this "getting hot," and it is not hard to recognize. I had it in 1982 in setting an NFL record with twenty straight completions against Houston. I was reading all of the defenses properly and so were my receivers; their routes were run exactly; our line blocked perfectly; my mechanics of ball handling and throwing were smooth, effortless and error-free; and my receivers made some astounding catches. When this is happening, everything looks wide open and easy to hit; defensive backs just miss knocking away passes and they become receptions; guys make diving catches; and tipped passes become completions, not interceptions. When the films come on, the first reaction is, "Boy, I put the ball into some tight holes, but they sure didn't look that tight when I was throwing it." I guess it is like a hitter in baseball going on a torrid streak where he hits over .400 for ten or twelve days. I have heard some of these players say that the ball looks as big as a balloon coming up to the plate and they can just pulverize it. Yet it is the same size ball, coming up to the plate the same way, when they go into a hitting slump. They cannot explain the difference, and really neither can a quarterback.

Rather than try to explain it, all of us wish that it could happen more often, but that never is the case. So the key is to recognize the occasional symptoms and then take advantage of them. There is a delicate balance to maintain, not doing too little and not doing too much, either of which can cool off that hot hand. When a team gets hot and jumps to a good lead, a quarterback, or his coach, should not become conservative or try to "sit" on the clock and be content with the points on the board. This is like throwing water on a fire, because the team suddenly goes away from the things that lit this fire, and everyone seems to back away and play with less enthusiasm. So many games, at every level of competition, are lost each year because teams stop doing what is successful and, in effect, forcibly change their personality. The Dr. Jekyll–Mr. Hyde routine then becomes a horror show in reverse.

At the same time, when the quarterback is zinging along and the team is rolling up some points, he cannot do foolish things, such as taking extraordinary risks that could result in an interception or making a bad play that could hand the momentum back to the opposition. The answer lies somewhere in between: continue to play with the same intensity and certainty that turned on the team, and play as though the score is tied. This consistency not only can win the game at hand but also can have a carryover effect that will last for several weeks. I know that feeling because it happened to the Bengals during our 1981 drive to the Super Bowl. In an eight-game stretch, we won seven games and outscored our opponents, 259–133; and that included five straight victories over some of the best NFL teams, in

155

which we outscored the opposition, 177–90. Nearly everything we did then was successful, and it was one of the most exciting times of my career, to know that I could go out and feel that our team would have a big day—and then to see it happen.

I guess I appreciated it all the more because I also had seen the not-so-pleasant times when I had to operate under adverse conditions. Here, the biggest battle is often within the quarterback himself. When things are not going well, the natural inclination is to try to make something positive happen. That is good. What is bad is trying to make something good happen by making a bad play.

There is some mental discipline involved here, by both the coach and the quarterback. I can get a team back on track easiest by doing the things that have the best opportunity to succeed—not forcing the ball into tight areas but swinging it to receivers who quickly come open and, as we noted earlier in the book, allowing the offensive line to come off the ball as a unit with the running game, and taking some short completions. A quarterback can begin to string some first downs together, get his team moving and build confidence, after which he can open up the offense a bit.

I have developed my own method of forestalling such down times by trying to get off to a good start at the beginning of a game. If I can get a couple of completions in the first series of plays, it calms me down and gets the team moving and into a good rhythm. I may use shorter-range passes or plays that I really feel confident will work against the defenses we are facing that day. Sometimes we may spring something we have especially cooked up for that team right at the start and get everyone revved up.

One year against the Raiders we started a receiver named John McDaniel, who, because he had been injured and had not played too much, was not in any of the film exchanges we made with the Raiders. He really was a burner, and we felt that he could go deep against Willie Brown, their great cornerback, who was in the late stages of his career. On the game's first play, we put John on Willie, man-for-man, went deep with the ball, and he made a big play that set up our first touchdown. That really picked us up and we stayed in the good groove for the rest of the game.

If it comes down toward the end of a game and the team is struggling to get a tie or a victory, then a quarterback must take a few more chances. However, he must know the situation—if all he needs is a field goal, then he should work on getting the ball into field-goal range. The worst play is to get greedy and go for a touchdown by forcing a bad pass and having the ball picked off. Result: no field goal, no touchdown, no victory. If the team needs a touchdown, then the quarterback must take more chances, go into the end zone with the ball and fire it into tighter holes. If it gets picked off, it gets picked off, but he can walk off the field secure that he had tried to get the victory with the best possible play.

Until that last play in those situations, the quarterback should keep plugging along, staying with the basics and allowing the defense and special teams to do their share. This is when the quarterback may be most tempted to try to do it all himself with the "big play," and that is the last thing he should be thinking about at that time. Even if he completes a big pass, it may mean nothing unless he can use it to get his team moving. If there still is enough time in the game, he is better off working with high-percentage plays that will produce some momentum, and then try for the big play as part of an overall offensive plan.

A good example occurred in another game against the Raiders when neither Kenny Stabler nor I was having a particularly good day on a rainy Sunday in Cincinnati. So I just kept working to try to make something positive happen. Near the end of the first half, Charlie Joiner broke toward the post, and Oakland had no free safety in its defensive coverage, so I hit Charlie at the five-yard line. That set up the winning touchdown, and a bad day turned into a good one only because we kept plugging along and did not do anything that would make an already bad day any worse.

This is not to say that a quarterback or coach should be timid about taking a big shot and perhaps getting a quick score late in the game when the team needs a couple of touchdowns to catch up. But the play should have a solid chance of succeeding. When we played the Jets in the 1982 playoffs and trailed, 30–17, early in the fourth quarter, I used the first play of a series to hit Cris Collinsworth on a deep sideline pass for an apparent touchdown, but it was called back because we were offside. Had it succeeded, it would have gotten us right back into the game with plenty of time still to win. But in selecting that play, we were almost certain that it would succeed because of the way the Jets had been playing their defense against us in that particular situation.

Still, that mistake took away our last real chance to win the game, and this brings us to a rather touchy situation: How does a quarterback react during a game when one of the players errs, particularly if it costs a big play?

I look at it two ways. First, was the mistake physical or mental? Physical mistakes are part of the game, and if they occur while the player is going all-out, there really is not too much to be said. Mental mistakes are something else, because often that goes back to a lack of preparation. If the player does not want to take the time to prepare, then why is he even playing? Now if the player normally is mistake-free and he blows a call, that also is something that can happen to anyone and I can excuse it. One reason is that when I throw an interception the players don't react adversely toward me. If the mistake involves a wrong pass route or a missed blocking assignment or something else to do with a specific play, then I try to get it worked out as quickly as possible so it will not be repeated.

Early in my career I saw a pro quarterback chewing out his blockers after he had been sacked, and it struck me that doing that, before a national television audience, did not seem to inspire them to protect him any better. I never was chewed out by my blockers for throwing an interception, so I decided that if someone did miss a block, I would tell them nicely not to let it happen again if they can help it. My blockers work hard for me and they don't deliberately get beaten on a pass rush, and if it does happen they feel worse about it than I do, so I certainly am not going to make that physical mistake a personal affront.

Where I get upset is if the guy makes the same mental mistake over and over, or if we have just gone over something and he goes out on the field and blows his assignment. That happened in a game against the Raiders (why do so many good and bad things always seem to happen against the Raiders, I wonder?) in a Monday night game where we asked one of our receivers to run a specific pattern in a special situation that we had worked on during the week, and reviewed it again just before it was called. But the player then ran the wrong pass route and the ball was intercepted. When I returned to the bench I lost my cool and chewed him out. I had never done that, though if a player is making the same mistake after we try to correct it, then I will firmly remind him how the play should be run. That is within the scope of a quarterback's leadership responsibility, and his players will respect him because the mistake is hurting them as a team.

Even here a quarterback must be careful how he makes the point. He should not pound the guy atop his helmet or push him around, or yell and scream so that it attracts everyone's attention. I never want to embarrass someone publicly, but I will not hesitate to at least say, "Let's get it done right," after again pointing out the error. The quarterback should know his personnel and which guys can take criticism and which guys are sensitive to it. Then it becomes a matter of how the criticism is delivered, not *whether* it is delivered.

Quarterbacks also must be capable of coping with other distractions during a game. The most difficult sometimes is the weather—heat and cold, rain, wind and snow, wet and icy playing surfaces. They must make some adjustments depending upon the bad weather situation, but they never can use the weather as an excuse, because during a career, a quarterback will have played well under bad conditions and poorly under good conditions. It boils down to going onto the field, despite the weather, and finding a way to function.

Our team proved that in the AFC championship game against San Diego after the 1981 season when the wind-chill factor made it feel like 59 degrees below zero at Riverfront Stadium. Before the game, our coach, Forrest Gregg, told us, "It will be a lot like going to the dentist. You know it's going to hurt, but you've got to go anyway." All of us dressed as warmly as we could, but then our offensive linemen donned short-sleeved jerseys and made it look like just another day as we won, 27–7. The poor Chargers, coming from warm California, never could adjust mentally to that bitter cold, and it showed in their poor performance.

In my experience, the longer you play football, the less you tend to worry about the weather, because you know the game is not going to be called off, so you might as well play it to the best of your ability. At the same time, a quarterback must learn to use the adverse conditions to his advantage. For instance, at Riverfront Stadium, I know where the slippery spots are on our artificial surface, so our receivers are a bit more conscious of those areas than opposing defensive backs, and we often have made some big plays because of them. In Cleveland, where there is natural grass at one end of the field and a dirt infield at the other, I know the latter will be more treacherous under bad conditions than the grass, so I will tailor what I do to take advantage of that condition. Of course, the Browns' defense knows it too, so it becomes a game of who can be the most clever.

Of all the weather conditions, wind is the worst. For one thing, a very windy day often means that there is only half a game to fully utilize the offense; the other half is spent working against the wind and trying not to make a mistake. The defense knows this, so the wind acts as a sort of legal twelfth man on the field. This is not an impossible situation, but it requires some mental discipline to tone down the offense until the conditions are favorable and then try, within two quarters, to utilize as much of the game plan as possible.

Rain is usually not a serious factor, but it is important not to disregard the weather report if it calls for a downpour during the game. If heavy rain is predicted, then we will be prepared to use two tight ends and a fullback to try to control the ball; and I will not force a slippery ball into a crowd. The power game avoids mistakes which give the opposition a cheap score. Of course, do not completely ignore the deeper patterns, but utilize them in situations where the defense has become vulnerable in the way they react to the short game, or set up an individual matchup so the receiver can suddenly change a technique that he has used for several plays and leave the defensive back spinning in his tracks.

By and large, rain is not too much of a factor. If there are enough footballs so that a dry one can be used for every play, then throwing the ball is not affected too much. I would add one other point: Be sure the footwear is suitable for the playing conditions and the field so that the drop-back and movement with the ball will be as smooth as possible.

Snow is something else, since a snowy field means a treacherous playing surface. Game plans often go out the window under these conditions, and if a team can get a good lead before the footing becomes too bad, it generally can win the game.

One advantage for the quarterback is that a snowy field cuts down the pass rush, so if a receiver can get open, there is a good chance that he can get the ball. I recall a game against the Steelers several years ago when we were ahead, 3–0, at the half and it began to snow heavily. As the second half evolved, the footing got worse and worse, but the Steelers scored and led, 7–3, when we got the ball for the last time.

I had found in those conditions that rather than tiptoeing back to the pocket, it was better for me to move fast and get more time to throw; Pittsburgh's great defensive line simply was not getting the traction it needed to mount a serious pass rush. In our final series, I hit a couple of big passes to get to their twenty-yard line with time for just one more play. We had called a time-out and I looked over at the Steelers' huddle and saw Joe Greene, their great tackle, removing his shoes and socks so he could get better traction. Joe never did get to me, and my pass to Chip Myers was just tipped away at the last second in the end zone. Still, I will never forget "Mean Joe" taking off his shoes and socks on the snowy field and lining up in his bare feet. It was the ultimate in frustration for him to have to play under such conditions.

Cold weather should not be a serious problem because football is an autumn-winter game and most players prefer cold days to the hot ones early in the season. Quarterbacks should take every precaution not to allow their hands to get too cold because, once it happens, you never seem able to warm up. One of our players will wear a pair of padded mittens while I am in the game so that I will have a warm pair to put on when I come to the sidelines. Playing, even on that minus 59-degree wind-chill day, seems to obscure the cold, and I never really pay much attention to it while I am on the field. I usually stick my hands down the front of my pants to allow my body heat to warm them between plays, though after one cold day several years ago, Coach Brown came to me and said, "We'll put a pouch in your jersey for the next game."

"Well," I replied, "I'd rather not use a pouch, Coach, because there is no warmth in there."

He did not press the matter, though I think he felt it looked a little funny on television.

Try not to overdress for the cold; wear only what is absolutely necessary. Too much clothing can impede a player's movements and can also cause heavy perspiration, even on the coldest days. Wet clothing on a freezing day is the best way to get frostbite, and besides that, it is most uncomfortable.

Regardless of the weather conditions, quarterbacks still are responsible for the manner in which they handle the ball. A cold day means a harder ball; a wet day means a slippery one. So the quarterback should spend a little bit more time in taking the snap to be sure it is secure, then be sure that it is firmly gripped when making the handoff. In passing it, he should be sure the receiver has a good ball to catch, one that is in front of him or into his body where he will not have to make too many moves in trying to catch it.

If a ball is very wet, I will not throw it as hard because it tends to slip as it is released. A softer throw will alleviate that problem. On a windy day, the ball must be thrown hard, and it is imperative to throw as tight a spiral as possible so the wind will not affect its flight too much. Receivers who are mentally tough and concentrate well on every ball that is thrown to them— we have a good group of that kind—will be able to make the catch in bad conditions.

Sometimes the worst weather conditions can seem rather tame in the face of hostile crowds. A crowd, home or away, can be a distraction, and long before a quarterback reaches professional football, he should learn to cope with it. If he comes from a small school, as I did, and never saw more than a few thousand fans at a game, then coming into a major-league stadium with sixty thousand fans screaming on nearly every play can be quite an experience and something that a player from a small school must cycle into his learning process. It is the same for a young man who goes from high school to a major college where he will be facing large crowds each week.

A home crowd, really cheering for their team, can pick up a player and inspire a team. It probably is most noticeable when the team is struggling during a game and suddenly everyone is on their feet, clapping, whistling and chanting. Then the adrenaline begins to flow and helps the team to get going. It has happened to us so many times, so I truly believe that the home crowd can help determine the outcome of a game.

The flip side is when the home folks begin to boo, particularly if the booing begins the moment the team comes out of its locker room to begin the game. That doesn't do anything to help, though crowds are fickle. Do something good and those boos are forgotten in the crescendo of cheers that begin cascading from the stands.

Quarterbacks should always remember that, like coaches, they are natural targets for the boo-birds, particularly if they are the starting quarterback and are having a bad game. The fans may start to scream for the backup, and if he doesn't do the job, then they will yell for the third quarterback. The third-string guy probably has it the best because the top two always are thrown into an adversary position in the view of the fans, and fans are pretty quick to let you know how they feel if things are not going right. The first thing the quarterback must learn is to win or face the music. During my career, I have become hardened to it, but not so much that it does not bother me. It bothers everyone who has pride in his work.

Away from home, the advantage obviously goes to the opposition, but the quarterback still can have the last word and silence that crowd very quickly with some good plays. Actually, it is a neat feeling to go into some place like Cleveland, which really supports its team and which has quite a rivalry with the Bengals, and silence a crowd of seventy thousand very quickly with some sustained offense. That, of course, lessens the noise distraction for a quarterback.

One touchy area is when fans begin to make an excess amount of noise as the quarterback prepares to call his signals at the line of scrimmage. As I noted early in the book, when this happens I simply keep my hands under the center and tell the umpire, who is directly in front of me and behind the defensive line, that I cannot hear and ask him to stop the clock. Again, I will not lift up until I see him make the time-out signal.

Away crowds really don't like this, and they often raise the decibel level when the quarterback tries again to have the ball snapped. But it is a situation that must be endured because the offensive linemen and backs must be able to hear the signals. If it continues, often the opposition players will raise their hands and ask their fans to be quiet, and that often does the trick. But a quarterback should *not* try to be a nice guy and go ahead under those noisy conditions just to get the crowd off his back.

In the NFL, some stadiums are worse than others, depending upon crowd size, the intensity of the rivalry, the importance of the game, and even the configuration of the stadium. In Baltimore, for example, one end zone is hugged by the enclosed part of Memorial Stadium; hence the fans seem almost on top of you at the end of the field. Those great Baltimore teams of John Unitas and Bert Jones used the noise as their own psychological weapon because it intimidated some teams. Late in the first half of a game we played there several years ago, I scrambled up the middle, and as I was hit and fell to the ground, the ball popped loose. Some Baltimore players jumped on it, but the officials ruled that the play was dead before the fumble, so we kept possession of the ball. That decision did not please the Colts' fans, and they became so noisy and unruly at that enclosed end of the field that a couple of officials wanted to declare the first half over, and then tack on the remaining thirty seconds to the second half. The referee wouldn't allow it, and we finally settled for a field goal to end the half.

The final thing a quarterback must cope with during a game is his own coach. I do not say this to be disrespectful or put down any coach, including my own. The burden really is on the player to endure any criticism, particularly after a mistake or a bad play. The worst thing is to get into a shouting match on the sidelines, but if emotions do get heavy, and under some conditions this can be unavoidable, hopefully both the quarterback and the coach are mature enough to allow it to go in one ear and out the other; and after it happens, everything is forgotten and both continue as before.

A coach, too, has to keep his cool and know when and where to be emotional. Most of the good ones are under control. If they do get upset, it is almost always justified, and the quarterback should pause, accept the criticism, evaluate what has been said, and not make the same mistake again.

Forrest Gregg, who was a fiery, emotional guy when he coached the Bengals, handled himself very well in this regard, but he always told us, "If you can't handle the pressure of a coach being critical, how can you handle the pressure out on the field when you are trying to win a game?"

That can apply to everything we have discussed in this chapter.

Chapter 7
Strategy—When and How

ALL that we have discussed till now regarding the necessity for thorough preparation, precise mechanics of ball handling and passing, and the proper mental and emotional balance during a game are but the prelude to allowing the quarterback to function as error-free as possible. His success then will come down to just how well he and his coaches can cope with all of the changing situations that the opposition and the game's circumstances will present.

This begins with utilizing the philosophy that his coach has decided will succeed. Will it be pass-oriented or run-oriented, and how will either best be used? The quarterback then must be able to read the multiple kinds of defenses he is likely to see—the zone, the man-for-man, the double zone, the combination coverages utilizing both zone and man-for-man and special-situation defenses such as the nickel alignment. Moreover, he also must know how to attack each defense with the correct play, in the safest, yet most productive manner, keeping in mind at all times such variable factors as down and distance, the frequency with which he uses each play, and his use of audibles. He then must know whether to use the run to set up his passing game, or vice versa, and which formation to use. Will it be one with two tight ends, two wide outs and a single setback? Or a conventional pro set with two setbacks, a tight end and two wide outs? And which will be most effective against the various defenses? He must know, too, how to mix and match this group to force special coverages which will give him an advantage.

The quarterback also has to be aware of the special "gadget" plays in his game plan and when will be the best time to use them, because normally they are one-shot deals. If his team falls behind by a couple of touchdowns, he may be asked to run a hurry-up offense in the fourth quarter to lessen the time advantage of the opposition; and if there still is a chance to win or tie within the last two minutes, he must have that two-minute drill firmly fixed. And finally if his team is leading, yet in possible danger of being caught, then he must know how to run out the clock and preserve the victory.

Other than that, he has nothing to worry about during the game!

Seriously, all of the foregoing is a very tall order for any quarterback, but it is within the scope of his responsibility—and possibility—during a game. If there is any question as to why I have stressed the need to prepare and to maintain poise under pressure, just being able to competently handle all that I have just described should be reason enough to work diligently to master the position.

The level of competition will decide just how many of these burdens a quarterback must assume. In professional football, every situation is applicable, and depending upon the level of college competition, there is not much that can be omitted, either. In high school, the sophistication certainly is not as clear-cut, and it would not be fair to expect a young lad, just beginning to learn about playing quarterback, to have all of these points within his grasp. It is far better that the quarterbacks on this level begin building the basics of the position and gradually—as they expand into tougher areas of competition—become more adept at some of the more varied responsibilities that await them. Every pro quarterback began this way, and the success that so many of them have achieved clearly shows that the task is not impossible.

Regardless of what offensive plans a coach and quarterback concoct for a game—and I am including the coach here, because many control the flow of a game by dispatching each play, offensively and defensively—the ultimate success depends upon the quarterback's ability to read the defensive coverage. The three basic coverages are zone and double zone, man-for-man, and combination zone and man-for-man; in addition there are special-situation alignments such as the "nickel" or extra defensive backs. We shall look at each in order, what they are, how to recognize them and then how to attack them.

ZONE: The zone defense protects certain areas of the field, and defensive players have responsibilities only for any receivers coming into these areas. Each zone has a "seam," which separates the various zones, or areas between each defender. In professional football, we have the harsh marks directly down the field in line with the goalpost uprights, so these become good markers in reading whether or not the defense will be zone, man-for-man, or double zone. When I am retreating to pass, I focus my vision straight down the middle of the field and watch both safeties. Their actions will give me a clue, and then so will the actions of the linebackers. If they drop back to cover an area of the field, then I know I am facing a zone defense; if they move up to cover a running back or tight end, then I can look for some form of man-for-man coverage.

Once the quarterback determines that he will be facing zone coverage, then he must know which kind. There are four:

Strong-side zone: Three defensive backs and two linebackers will move toward the strong side of our offensive formation—where the tight end and flanker are located—to protect their areas of responsibility. A good key is whether the weak safety—the safety lined up on the side where there is only a split end—stays in the middle of the field. A team that utilizes a strong passing game toward the strong side of its offensive formation can expect to face a lot of strong-side zone coverage.

Weak-side zone: The defensive backs and linebackers will move toward the weak side of the offensive formation away from the tight end and flanker. If the strong safety moves toward the center of the field and the weak safety moves into an area on the weak side of the formation, then the quarterback faces the weak-side zone; and he can expect to see quite a bit of that coverage if he has a very effective receiver working from the weak side.

STRONG-SIDE ZONE

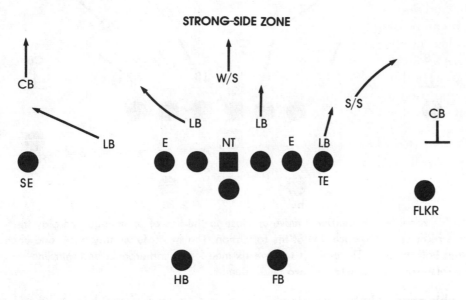

Strong-side zone: This defense is set to the strong side of the offensive formation, or the side where the tight end and flanker are positioned. Note the cornerback and safety to that side, plus the two linebackers and the other safety, all play to that side of the field and move to designated "drop" areas.

WEAK-SIDE ZONE

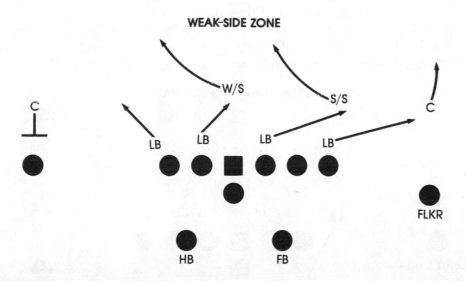

Weak-side zone: The strength of this zone defense favors the weak side of the offensive formation, or the side where the split end is positioned. The linebackers on that side of the offensive formation, plus the cornerback and safety, all will move to protect areas on that side of the formation.

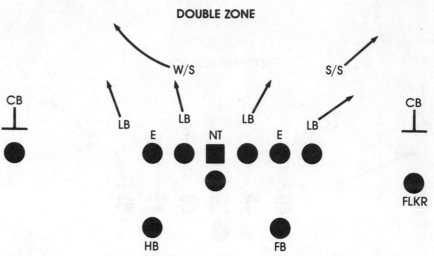

DOUBLE ZONE

Double zone: Both cornerbacks move up close to the line of scrimmage and play the wide receivers set to each side of the formation. The two safeties stay back, and each plays half the field. The effect is to have six men—two cornerbacks and four linebackers—across the field and two backs deeper.

Double zone: Both cornerbacks will come up and play the wide receivers on each side of the offensive formation, and the safeties will stay back and each will play half of the field, rather than having three defensive backs move to their areas of responsibility; so in effect the defense will have six men across the field, and two (the safeties) deep.

Combination: This is part zone defense, part man-for-man. The key usually is the action of the linebackers. If they move to cover the tight end or running backs, after the safeties have made their move, then the quarterback knows that he will face a weak- or strong-side zone on one side of the field, and probably some form of man-for-man coverage on the other side.

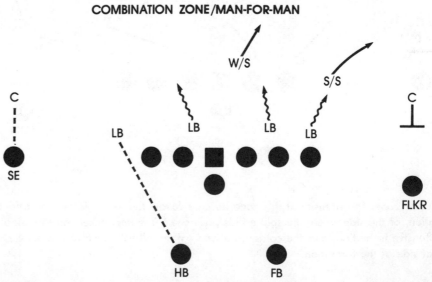

COMBINATION ZONE/MAN-FOR-MAN

Combination zone/Man-for-man: The safeties will first make a move to cover a designated area, and the linebackers will move to cover the tight end and/or the running backs. The side of the field covered by the safeties will be a zone defense, and the movement of the linebackers will clue the man-for-man coverage responsibilities.

With the continued efforts of the defense to take away some of the built-in advantages that the offense enjoys, there is greater use of varied offensive formations. It is not unusual for a team to use as many as two or three dozen different formations in a game, which means that the defenses are constantly seeing the weak side and strong side being changed as the play is being called. For instance, a team could come up to the line of scrimmage in the standard I formation, with a flanker and tight end on the right and an end split out to the left, meaning that its strong side is to the right. One of the I backs could shift into the slot between the tackle and the split end, thus showing the defense two receivers on either side of the formation. Or it has become fashionable to utilize two tight ends, two wide outs and one setback. If everyone lines up accordingly, there is no strong or weak side, yet the offense can declare one by sending either one of the tight ends or wide outs in motion, and forcing the defense to change its coverage. We will look at this closer as we discuss the use of various formations, and what reactions a quarterback can expect from the defense.

Once a quarterback recognizes one of the zone formations, how should he go about attacking it?

The first commandment is to be patient. The quarterback should be willing to dig and dunk a bit because the whole concept of a zone defense is to keep the offense from biting off huge chunks of yardage at a time; rather, it almost is a calculated risk on the defense's part that it will grudgingly give up bits of the field—if it must give up anything—and figures that sooner or later over a long march, and for a dozen or more plays, the offense will either make a mistake or break down and have to punt.

Knowing that, the quarterback should look for those areas *underneath* the zones, or between the zones, and if his offensive line can provide him with enough time, watch his receivers expand the zones being covered and then look for receivers in the open seams between those ever-expanding areas. Further, if the quarterback sees the defense going into weak-side zone coverage, he should then look to the strong side, where there will be more room and fewer defenders; and of course, vice versa, if the defense goes into strong-side coverages. The tough one is the *double zone rotation*, where the corners and safeties cover each side of the field. Hopefully he will have a receiver going down the middle, which is the vulnerable area in that coverage with no defensive back moving there for coverage responsibility.

A quarterback can attack the zone defense with his running and passing game, the latter being used, as we have noted earlier, with play-action after having established a good running attack. An example is to hold the linebackers with the play-action fake and then send the receivers into the areas they normally would cover before they can get back into those zones. Regardless of what plan is made, it is important to spread the field and make the defense cover every inch of it, stretching their zones of responsibility thin enough for there to be openings for the receivers. How best to do that?

With the running game: Against a strong-side zone, the strong safety usually has the responsibility to play the run and turn it inside, so it makes sense to run toward the weak side; and the opposite is true against weak-side zone coverage. Against double rotation, the cornerbacks on both sides usually have the responsibility to come up quickly and force the run into the middle.

ATTACKING UNDER/BETWEEN/OVER ZONES

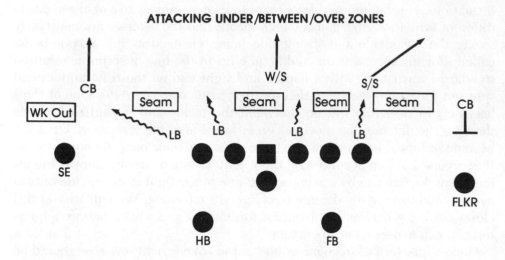

Attacking the zones: The soft spots, or "seams," of the zone defense are indicated by the squares under and between the various drop areas. Receivers will work to get into these areas and between the defenders. When the quarterback works against a double rotation in the zone defense, he will usually see three large "seams" between the areas patrolled by the safeties.

ATTACK DOUBLE ROTATION

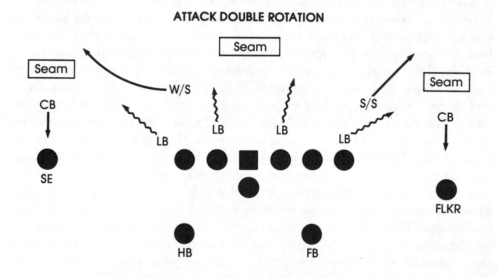

That leaves the linebackers. The linebackers and defensive line always work in concert to help contain the running game, and the secondary is the final line of defense. If a team can establish a good running attack, it will not be long before the entire defense becomes preoccupied with it, and thoughts of pass defense become a bit fuzzy. The secondary and linebackers will begin to creep up to get to the runners, and that will leave more and more room behind them, which then becomes open country for receivers.

Of course, an effective passing attack against any defense also will loosen up the defense and make it more vulnerable for the running game. While the quarterback is the key operator in recognizing the zone, the responsibility for getting open within the zones or along their seams falls directly upon the pass receiver. All the hipper-dipper moves in the world really do not mean too much because the defenders are not covering a specific receiver—they are covering an area, so it is up to the receiver to find the open areas on the field.

There are ways to do that. If the quarterback spots a strong-side zone defense, he can throw weak-side pass patterns, with a halfback stopping in the area between two linebackers, the split end curling in behind the linebacker, and the tight end going into the middle between defenders. The quarterback also can have a running back coming into an area in front of a linebacker to influence his movements—"clearing out," is the popular expression—and then have the split end come into that area. This is where a good comeback pattern is effective.

While this philosophy of being patient and taking what the defense is willing to give is sound, I will not totally ignore the long pass. For example, if a team plays the strong-side zone, a split end with great speed has a chance to blow past the weak corner. If the quarterback plans to throw over the middle, he should have someone going down the middle to occupy the weak safety so the receiver can work in front of him. The ideal is to have receivers in the short range, the intermediate range and the deeper range to stretch out those zones, and then go to whichever guy is open.

There are many times when a quarterback will discover that zone defenses are "playing plays"—that is, anticipating that one receiver will be targeted for the pass. This happens when teams meet a couple of times a season and become familiar with each other's plays. So they play the play within the zone, ignoring other receivers. A receiver's information can be invaluable if he tells the quarterback that he is not being played "honestly" by the defense. That is a good time to fake one of those plays that the defense is anticipating, and then bring another receiver into the area that has been vacated. Suddenly, there may be nothing but wide open spaces after the ball has been caught.

MAN-FOR-MAN DEFENSE: Some coaches call this the purest and the best method of pass defense. Rather than moving to predetermined areas of the field for coverage, the two cornerbacks are assigned to cover the two wide receivers; the tight end will be covered by the safety and the linebacker facing him; the two running backs will be covered by the other two linebackers; and the other safety will patrol the middle of the field, with the responsibility of helping either of the two cornerbacks.

This was the kind of coverage most NFL teams played in the fifties and sixties, until the American Football League teams popularized the bump-and-run and the zone alignments. Since there were only a dozen pro teams until 1960, the NFL teams could select the best athletes as defensive backs because this defense requires swift, sure athletes who can shadow other swift, sure athletes. Defensive backs must have trigger-sharp reactions that

171

make them stop, go, turn, come back or run step-for-step with the fleetest wide receivers. If a team has three or four defensive backs with these characteristics, and can place a solid pass rush in front of them, then the opposing quarterbacks will face long afternoons. The great pro teams that successfully used man-for-man pass coverage, such as the Giants, Lions and Packers of the fifties and sixties, all had outstanding defensive lines which put relentless pressure on quarterbacks and forced them to throw before their receivers could free themselves of the man-for-man coverage. It was as true then as it is today that if a quarterback has enough time to throw, then a receiver can beat any kind of coverage.

How does a quarterback determine whether the pass coverage will be zone or man-for-man?

A good first key that a quarterback can check as he is calling the signals is the position of the cornerbacks. In man-for-man coverage they generally will play a bit tighter to the line of scrimmage because they will have to cover a specific man wherever he goes, and they do not want him to get away from them too quickly. The second, as already noted, is the action of the linebackers after the ball is snapped, as they move directly to cover a running back or a tight end. In zone coverage, the linebackers will move directly on an angle to protect an area. In man-for-man, they will move sideways to pick up the running back coming from the backfield, or at least check his movements before going to help on other coverage. If the backs stay in to block, the linebackers generally will help the cornerbacks, or stay close to the line of scrimmage in case one of the backs suddenly should be released as a receiver.

Unless a quarterback knows that the people who play man-for-man defense are exquisite athletes, he may lick his chops at the prospect of working against it, particularly if his personnel are as talented as those the Bengals have had over the past few seasons. A big advantage is isolating a running back on a linebacker because there are few linebackers who can match the speed and elusiveness of a good running back. The wide receivers can utilize the "move" patterns, such as the post-corner or shake, the down-and-outs and the down-and-ins, and the crossing patterns. All of these are designed to give the receiver a step or two on the defender, and then get him going into open territory. The crossing pattern and the shake are two of the best because they get people running across the field and a quarterback can lay the ball up and allow the receiver to run under it.

I do not mean to imply that this is easy pickings because the greatest danger to a quarterback is the free safety. He patrols the middle of the field and expects the cornerbacks to funnel the receivers into his area. Hence, a receiver freeing himself by a step or two of the corner and heading across the field will then be picked up by the free safety. Free safeties are clever guys because they are not reckless about their coverage. If one reads the quarterback's eyes and sees him watching a particular receiver, that clue will send him to that man.

This is just an added burden for the quarterback. Obviously, he cannot throw the ball to a spot that he is not watching, yet at the same time he should not stare down a receiver from the moment he leaves the line of scrimmage. It is a natural reaction for quarterbacks at all levels—I have found myself doing it too much sometimes—to watch that primary receiver.

We have a progression type of passing game, so I will look at each one or, as I noted, perhaps only at the first one if he is open. All good quarterbacks will develop a habit of looking one way, then another, and coming back to find the open receiver. Much depends upon the play system, but every QB should concentrate on not betraying his patterns with constant eye contact. I will outline a drill in the next chapter that will help to alleviate this problem, but it also is as much mental as it is physical.

Success in working with wide receivers against man-for-man coverage depends on finding the single coverage. That often is a cat-and-mouse game played by the cornerback and free safety, and that game lasts only as long as the quarterback's protection keeps away the pass rush and allows him enough time to pick out an open receiver. Many man-for-man defenses will feature combination coverages beside the cornerback and safety. Sometimes they will use two safeties, particularly if the tight end is swift and strong, or the linebacker and strong safety; or they may use two linebackers to double cover a running back if the other back stays in to block. It is the passer's responsibility to sift through these various combinations to try to select the receiver with only single coverage; and it is equally important for every receiver to try to free himself and give the quarterback an open target.

SPECIAL-SITUATION DEFENSES: The most common form is the nickel defense, in which an extra defensive back replaces one of the linebackers in obvious passing situations. Some teams take it farther, inserting two defensive backs (that's a "dime" defense), and it has become not uncommon to see seven backs in the game at one time. With so many pass defenders, it gets very difficult to read specific coverages, because there are so many people doing so many different things.

There is no blanket set of rules that apply to the nickel back's responsibilities, which is why the quarterback must be very careful in how he attacks

NICKEL DEFENSES

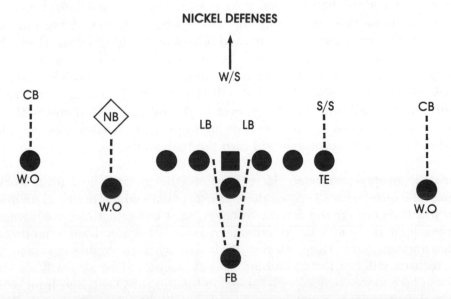

Nickel defense: This features a fifth, or nickel, back who is inserted into the secondary after a linebacker has been removed. The nickel back will play either zone or man-for-man coverage, and is generally meant to take away the long completion in a zone defense and to shadow a wide receiver when the defense goes man-for-man.

this defense. Often I wish matters were as cut and dried as in Atlanta a couple of years ago when the Falcons used two different nickel backs—one for zone coverage, the other for man-for-man. I needed only to check a jersey number to know what the coverage would be, and it worked well until the Falcons crossed us up by sending in the man-for-man guy to play zone. I threw an interception and learned, for the umpteenth time, that a quarterback can't get too smart and rely solely on what the scouting report says. What he sees the defense doing on the field must always be the determining factor.

Mostly, the nickel back will be used in zone coverage for long-yardage situations, and he usually will be used to take away the deep pass. On third-and-fifteen, there will not be too many holes in which to find an open receiver. Good preparation requires that a quarterback have a few special pass "packages" prepared for such instances, utilizing receivers on both sides of the coverage.

When the nickel back is in man-for-man coverage, the quarterback simply must find the receiver who has single coverage. Remember, there are seven pass defenders and as many as five receivers, so two of the receivers will have single coverage. Most teams will counter the nickel back by inserting a third wide receiver, sometimes four. That puts a great deal of pressure against the cornerbacks, and the defense still must cope with the tight end and perhaps a swift running back who easily can overmatch a linebacker. The key is to get as many receivers into the game as possible and put the pressure right back on the defense.

There are other instances during a game when the quarterback will be faced with special-situation defenses. Here are some of the more common:

Outside the twenty-yard line: When the quarterback is trying to protect a slim lead a defense often will gamble in trying to make a big play, force a turnover or get the ball in good field position for a time-efficient scoring drive. A defense may crowd the gaps in the line to prevent a big running play, or have a preset series of slants and blitzes by the linebackers. Here, the quarterback must take extra care to look at the defense while he is calling signals and recognize what might be coming. If he senses the blitz, he can check off the play to something that will give him the advantage; or if he is unsure, he can call time-out and go over to the sideline and discuss with his coaches upstairs what the defense is trying to present. Whatever he does, he must not make a mistake that will turn the ball over.

Inside the twenty-yard line: Here is where the football field itself works against the quarterback because there is less room in which to run an offense, thus less territory for the defense to cover, so it can effect closer coverage. For example, there may be no free safety, as such, because there is no threat of having him cover deep. So that back will work in double coverage. A quarterback will see more combination coverages and he also will see the defense take more chances with these combinations to keep him from scoring. A defense tries to negate many big plays with blitzes, and when the ball lands inside its twenty-yard line, it will blitz again, hoping not only to take away a possible touchdown but also to make a field goal more difficult.

A quarterback will see more man-for-man coverage once he gets inside the

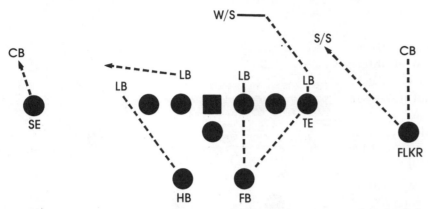

Special situation defense: Normally man-for-man coverages will be employed inside the twenty-yard line. The diagram indicates that the split end will be covered by the corner-back and linebacker on that side of the field; the outside linebackers will cover the running backs; the strong safety and cornerback will cover the flanker; and the tight end will be picked up by the other safety.

twenty-yard line, again because the field has become constricted. Here is where the running game can be very effective, if only because the defense will be thinking about the pass. A quarterback can use this influence by sending receivers toward one side of the field, and then handing off the ball for a run to the opposite side, with an opportunity for a big gainer. If the QB is faced with a long-yardage situation, even first-and-ten, a quick trap or draw, particularly with a very good running back, is a splendid weapon with which to cross up the defensive coverage.

If the offensive scheme calls for passing inside the twenty-yard line, a third wide receiver will be very effective, again because the defense cannot double cover everyone. Slick wide receivers, even operating within such restricted areas, can get free, and it is up to the quarterback to find them. However, there is no blanket set of rules that says a team must run a definite kind of play to produce points. On third-and-long, we have used a screen pass with as much effectiveness as we have used the draw play. We have succeeded with post-corner patterns, slants and square outs.

What we work hard to avoid is the mistake that either will turn the ball over and kill the scoring opportunity or will push us out of field-goal range. A sack can result from either a pass-blocking breakdown or a blitz. Quarter-backs should again be wary of the blitz and look for it before the ball is snapped; and they should not use patterns that cause their line to hold blocks for a long time, forcing either a holding call or a sack. With so little territory, the pass should be fairly quick—either it is there or it isn't. If it is, throw the ball; if it is not, throw the ball away.

Goal line: Here the defense rightly anticipates the running game, particularly if it is third- or fourth-and-one. In will come an extra linebacker or line-man, and a defensive back or two will leave. We always want to know when the opposition makes these special substitutions. Sometimes it may not be until the ball is inside the three-yard line, sometimes the two, maybe as far out as the five. But once they do, then that will dictate the special kinds of

175

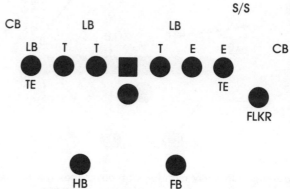

Special situation defense: Goal line. It has become common for a defense to use five linemen and one linebacker across the front when confronted with goal-line situations. The defensive linemen will play in the gaps between the offensive linemen, and one cornerback will face the tight end on the left side. The other cornerback will roll up close to the line of scrimmage to play the flanker, while the two linebackers will be close to the line to help with running plays or jump quickly into pass coverage in the end zone, along with the strong safety.

offense we can use. Obviously, if they take out a defensive back or two, the passing situation should be to the quarterback's advantage, but with so little ground in which to operate, it should be quick or not at all.

Defenses generally will play a gap defense, with their linemen taking a low charge at the spaces between the offensive line to knock off as many blockers as possible. The linebackers play close to stop the run. Matters become very basic in this situation, and an offensive lineman generally will fire out and try to knock his man off the line of scrimmage just enough to allow the back to wedge through. With the defensive line taking the low charge, often the play's success will be determined by a lead blocker coming in ahead of the ball carrier. That lead blocker must be able to get to the linebacker and knock him backward, or even off balance, just enough for the runner to crash over the goal line.

I guess goal-line situations always will have a special significance for me after our ill-fated venture in Super Bowl XVI where, trailing 20–7, we had a first down at the 49ers' three-yard line late in the third quarter. On first down, our fullback, Pete Johnson, got two yards to the one-yard line, a very good run considering the intensity of the game. On second down, with two tight ends and David Verser, a good blocking wide receiver, in the game, we decided to run Johnson to the left again. We brought David in motion so that he could peel off and block the outside linebacker, Jack Reynolds, but as I was calling signals, I noticed that Reynolds had moved his position directly into the area where the play was to be run. So with an audible, I changed Verser's route to allow him to lead the play into that area and get a direct shot at the linebacker.

Unfortunately, the noise level in the Silverdome was so intense that he failed to pick up the change and never altered his route. There was no one to block Reynolds, who knocked off our lead blocker, Charles Alexander, and middle linebacker Dan Bunz and tackle John Henry helped to stuff the play without a gain.

On third down, we used one of our goal-line passes, a toss to Alexander, who was to wait for Verser to get into the end zone and clear out the right side, after which Charley would sprint to the right and into the end zone and catch the pass. Unfortunately, David did not run the pattern deeply enough, so the area became crowded and Charley stayed just a yard outside the end zone as he ran his route. My pass was just a little behind him, forcing him to break his momentum somewhat in reaching for it. Bunz was able to catch up to the play before Alexander could get his body over the goal line and again we were stopped for no gain.

What still tortures me to this day was later seeing in the films that Dan Ross had sprinted across the defense and stood in the other side of the end zone without a defender within twenty-five yards. If Bunz had crowded Alexander just a little bit more, Ross was next on my progression list and I could have had the easiest touchdown pass of my life.

On fourth down, we again used a running play for Johnson, one that had succeeded more than 90 percent of the time, but the 49ers made a great defensive play. First they put three men over the center and this prevented Blair Bush from getting out to block Bunz. Our right tackle, Mike Wilson, actually moved his man off the line of scrimmage for a split second, but Bunz, unmolested, stepped in to knock off Alexander, our lead blocker, and the rest of the 49ers' defense swarmed to knock down Johnson. While we scored five minutes later to narrow the score to 20–14, that lost opportunity probably cost us the chance to achieve one of the most astounding comebacks in NFL championship game history; we always felt those were five minutes we could have used to score the winning touchdown.

One other key time when defenses can gang up on the offense is after a large penalty. Penalties, particularly the ten- and fifteen-yard varieties, are deflating to an offense, but they need not be deadening, particularly if the quarterback has two or three downs in which to come back. Let's look at some of the situations:

1. If the penalty gives the quarterback a first-and-twenty or first-and-twenty-five situation, then the key to recouping is to get something on the next play. In those situations, the defense will most likely bring in its nickel back and play a zone coverage. Therefore, the quarterback should not attempt to get everything back in one big gulp, but do something that will cut that yardage down, even by six or seven yards, by working the intermediate areas between the zones. Three seven-yard completions after a first-and-twenty will get a first down; a nine-yard completion and two eights will also get a first down after a first-and-twenty-five. But the key is to get something right away, to lessen that yardage figure and keep some pressure on the defense.

2. If it gets to be second or third down, with twenty or twenty-five yards to go, then, depending on field position, the quarterback must put the ball farther down the field. He should have people in the game who can make the longer plays—an extra wide receiver, a swift, good pass-catching running back. The danger is to make a bad situation even worse by forcing a throw into tough coverage and turning the ball over.

177

3. If it gets to be third down and less than ten, there may be more man-for-man coverage, so the quarterback can go to an individual pass route, such as the crossing pattern. If the situation is impossible, then he can at least chink out a few yards with a draw or a trap, and that can be added to what the punter can produce. Then allow the defense to take away the ball.

Knowing the various defenses, the situations in which they can be called and how best to attack them, what should the quarterback think about in calling a game, or in operating the game plan as it is called by the coaching staff?

There are certain principles that must be considered before discussing what to call in specific situations. Here are the principles I believe to be the most important:

1. *Personnel:* The people available really dictate the types of things a quarterback can do. If a team has a great running back, then it should feature him, regardless of the situation, because that kind of player is a threat to score a touchdown every time he touches the ball. That team obviously will feature the run as the major part of its offense, meaning that first downs will become running downs as will second-and-medium-yardage situations. If the team has great receivers and a good thrower, then first downs can be throwing downs, and the forward pass will become the offense's prime feature.

If a team does not have a good running game, or an outstanding runner, then for it to insist on making first down the running down often will bring up second-and-long, and the defense immediately goes into its nickel coverage. But get five, six or seven yards on a first-down pass, and the offense then dictates the kind of coverage the defense must use. The key is using people who will not put the offense in a hole from which escape is less than a fifty-fifty chance.

I am not pushing the pass as the primary weapon, though it is one that certainly has worked for me. Coaches, particularly at the college and high school levels, sometimes become unrealistic in trying to adapt it to their offense when they do not have either the personnel or an assistant who are fully versed in the concept of a well-organized pass play. Perhaps the team does not have a line coach who can teach pass blocking, without which no passing game ever will succeed. So the need for personnel reaches into both the playing and coaching levels.

Coaches also should be realistic about using their people. So often we hear about a "decoy," often a topflight receiver, to occupy defensive people while the quarterback tries to work with his other pass catchers. Unless that great player is subpar and the coach wants to restrict his physical contact, then using him as a "decoy" really is self-defeating, because the team simply takes away its best player. The key, then, is to find a way to use him, even knowing that the defense will give him special attention. We have seen that for years with Isaac Curtis, one of pro football's most feared wide receivers ever since he came into the league. Yet we never say, "Today, I am not going to throw to you because the defense will give you the most attention." We look for him always to be open, and if he is not, I throw to someone else who has less attention. Even so, we build into our game plans ways in which Isaac can get open and be a total part of our game. That is part of good planning.

2. *Field position:* If a team is backed up and a long third-down situation at hand, it is not a bad idea, as we noted, to hand off the ball, punt it out, and put the hat on the defense to get it back. However, if the ball is in on the forty-yard line and it is third-and-long, a ten-yard play can buy field-goal range. Then comes the question: Try for twenty yards and a first down, or try to get ten and set up the field goal? Obviously, it will be tough to get the twenty, but three points, unless a team is behind by a couple of touchdowns late in the game, never will hurt.

3. *Score and time to play:* If a team is behind by a touchdown or less, backed up deep in its territory and facing a third-and-long situation, the key is to not turn over the ball and give the opposition a cheap score that will put the game out of reach. Go ahead and run a high-percentage play; then if necessary, punt the ball and allow the defense to get it back for one last shot. If a team is behind by more than a touchdown and time is running out, the quarterback must throw to get a big play. If it is picked off, at least the quarterback can walk off the field knowing he was trying to win.

4. *Take what the rules give:* At every level, rules governing line blocking and chucking by defensive backs and linebackers favor the pass offense, so the offensive plays should take advantage of what the rules allow. This follows in selection of personnel. It is more desirable to have a quarterback who can throw than one who is strictly a runner. If he can do both, that is like money in the bank.

5. *Take advantage of defensive alignments:* Common sense applies here. For instance, if the quarterback calls a run to the strong side of his formation and then he sees the defense is stacked to that side, he should call an audible at the line of scrimmage. Even before the game, he should have discussed what plays are best run in such situations, so that he can easily make the change. Then the question is, run or pass? Okay, check the cornerbacks. Are they playing back, and does that open up a quick out pattern? If they are not, then what about a quick trap to the weak side of the defense? This is part of a quick mental checklist the quarterback can use before calling signals. The key, either way, is to keep himself from making a bad play, or needlessly beating his head against the wall. Find something that will work.

6. *Stay with a successful play until the defense finds a way to stop it:* A common sense approach, to be sure, but too often a coach will be afraid to try a successful play too many times, lest the defense finds a way to stop it. That is the defense's problem, and if it cannot cope, don't take it off the hook by looking for something that might not happen. In situations like this, we will run the same play but use different formations to give it a different look. Despite the play's different appearances, the defense still has the same problems in trying to cope. Any time one or two receivers have seven- or eight-catch days, then the defense could not cope with one or two particular plays, which it probably saw from several different formations.

7. *Frequency of plays:* This follows directly from plays that the defense cannot stop. If one of our backs is having a big day with one or two specific

179

plays, I will call those plays again and again until the defense stops them. In these instances, a defense often will bunch up to protect a soft area, and that is when the quarterback can make a big play elsewhere. When the defense falls back to protect itself, then I will go back to work on the vulnerable spots.

8. *Running to set up the pass, or passing to set up the run:* This depends upon a team's offensive philosophy. We feature the pass, and we often line up with one setback, two tight ends and two wide receivers. If we are successful passing, then the defense becomes vulnerable when we turn loose our fullbacks.

Before the one-back offense became popular in the early eighties, most pro teams used the two-setback formation or the I formation, and all of us still do for certain plays and situations. The two-setback formation, or pro set, was the standard in pro football well into the seventies. It can feature two setbacks split behind the quarterback, the fullback to the strong side of the formation, where he can be a lead blocker for plays going there, or he can get the ball himself for plays going back to the weak side, with the half-

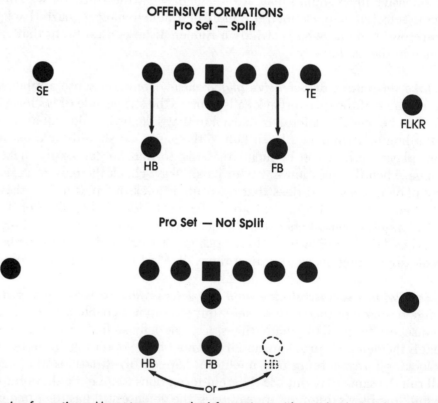

Offensive formations: Many teams use the I formation, with two backs lined up directly behind the quarterback, and a variation with just one back set deep. The standard pro set formations feature a split backfield, with the halfback lined up behind the offensive tackle on the weak side of the formation and the fullback behind the tackle on the other side. The variation features the fullback directly behind the quarterback and a halfback set to either side behind a tackle. In all formations, there are one tight end and two receivers split out to either side.

back as the lead blocker; or either back can get the straight handoff for dive or trap plays. This setup also is effective for passing, because both backs easily can flare out into their patterns, or they are in excellent position to act as pass blockers. Another pro set formation has the fullback lined up directly behind the quarterback and a halfback to one side or the other. This primarily is a running formation, with one back acting as blocker for plays between the tackles.

Many teams, ours included, use the I formation with two backs behind the quarterback. The linebackers cannot easily key on one back to get the ball, nor can they assume that a play is going to a particular side of the offense. The deep back, or the tailback, can get the ball deep in the backfield and has an opportunity to see what the defense is doing, and thus picks his holes. This is a particular advantage for shifty runners such as Marcus Allen, Wilbert Montgomery and Tony Dorsett. Some teams, such as Houston, will put their biggest runner—and few are bigger than Earl Campbell—deep in the I and allow him to get a running start so that, when he hits the hole, he is at full throttle. In reality, he is a fullback lined up as a halfback (with another fullback blocking for him), but no one bothers to argue about such technicalities when he comes charging through the line.

9. *Use of formations:*   We have already looked at the basic offensive formations which teams on every level will use, save for those who still favor the wishbone and veer systems. As we noted in discussing the ways to attack the nickel defense, using two good pass-catching running backs and inserting a third wide receiver for the tight end can create man-for-man coverage between one of the backs and a linebacker. Teams that use the two-back setup favor this.

Use of two tight ends, two wide outs and one setback will balance the defensive coverage because there is no strong or weak side. Unless there is additional shifting before the ball is snapped, everything is strong side, and depending on the approach, the quarterback always can use these formation changes to develop weak-side patterns with both strong-side alignments and thus attack the weak side of the defense. This also is a good running formation because it utilizes another good blocker.

The defense, meantime, often will declare one side to be the strong side in the way it stations its people against all alignments, so that one safety will automatically become the strong safety. That means the other safety must cope with our second tight end, and the cornerbacks have to match the wide receivers, with help only from the linebackers. That enables the offense to go into the weakness of the coverage.

Like many teams, we move our players about before the ball is snapped, and that is either to set up what we consider will be individual mismatches, or simply to add some confusion to the defense by not sitting in the same formation for ten seconds and allowing them to figure out what we are going to do. Much will depend on what we have seen of the defense's tendencies on film. Sometimes it will not react to any shifts, so that will allow us, for example, to take our tight end and move him from the strong side to the weak side. Some teams will place their best run linebacker, but a poor pass defender, against the tight end, and put the linebacker who defends best against the pass and not so well against the run on the other side. We may

181

flop our tight end to get him against the linebacker who has trouble with the pass, and thus get an advantage.

While all of this is happening, as we noted earlier in the book, the defense must keep track and alter any of its coverage schemes. Often you can catch it still trying to make the final adjustment when the ball is snapped and then get an instant advantage.

If the quarterback has a third wide receiver in the backfield and puts two wide receivers to one side of the formation and then shifts them to the other side, he may get a strong safety covering a wide receiver in a mismatch. There are other situations where, with two wide receivers on the same side, the defense will put its weak safety to cover the inside, or slot, man. By putting the best wide receiver on the formation's other side, he then may work against a strong safety who is not as fast nor as quick, and that brings still another mismatch. The quarterback should know, going into the game, just what the defensive tendencies will be and plan how he wishes to match them with his own personnel.

10. *How to start the game:*   Knowing and being prepared for all of the various situations that can happen, I still never have believed in wasting any plays, even at the beginning of a game. I will have the first three plays already set when I go into the game. While everyone has butterflies and needs a couple of plays to settle down—particularly in a crucial game—I believe in using high-percentage plays which can gain some yardage and get us going. Sixty percent of the time, our first play will be a pass. Why not? Let's fire at that defense, and go right after it from the start. We will use high-percentage passes that are easier to complete because they serve not only to get rid of the butterflies but also to build up the yardage and confidence and get everyone into the swing of the game. Field position obviously dictates this approach to some extent, and if we are backed up to our end zone after a short kickoff return, we will be a little more conservative with our opening plays than if we were out beyond the twenty-yard line.

All that we have discussed thus far pertains to all that can happen in the normal course of a game, but rare is the game that is normal, certainly not with the specialty defenses so rampant today. Rather, it always seems as if a quarterback is bumping against special situations. For instance, if it is second-and-fourteen, we noted that it is not necessary to try to get all fourteen yards in one play. If the defense brings in the nickel back and takes out a linebacker, that presents a mismatch, and there is an opportunity for a trap or draw play, where the smaller nickel back must take on a bigger back. Likewise, if the defense makes no substitution, then it is a good spot for a pass. But regardless of the decision, the quarterback must be aware at all times of the personnel that are facing him.

When a team is down by two or more touchdowns, it is not a bad idea to go to a *hurry-up offense*—a sort of early-bird two-minute drill—sometime in the second half to try to cut that deficit without using any time-outs or too much time. The key is to keep special defensive people off the field, with seven- and eight-yard gains on each play, and make the defense play with personnel that give the quarterback his best advantage, meaning that the defense cannot make the nickel substitution. This requires everyone to hustle on each play so the defense will not have time to substitute; the quarterback to use his audibles and be sure that everyone can hear them; and all players to exercise the discipline not to go offsides or move before the snap. The hurry-up offense should be planned and worked on before the game, so that when the decision is made, everyone is familiar with the plays to be used and quickly gets into the pace.

How is this different from the *two-minute offense?* First are the rules, such as when an injury will not stop the clock and will cost the team a time-out; that a fumble cannot be advanced except by the person who had possession of the ball; when the clock will be stopped and restarted, either at the ball's snap or on the signal of the referee; when the ball can be snapped (never with the umpire standing with his foot against it as he awaits the referee's signal to begin).

The quarterback must also look at the situation. Does he need a touchdown or a field goal? Or does he need more than one possession? In the last two minutes of the first half, the quarterback will take anything he can get. In any case, he should have at least two wide receivers in the game.

This is part of the game plan and knowing the coverages that the opposition favors in these situations. The quarterback must call his own plays unless there is a time-out when he can consult with the coaches. While some teams will call two plays at one time in the huddle, we audible ours one-at-a-time at the line of scrimmage because we can tailor each one to the situation and have a better opportunity of making the best possible call.

What is called depends on the defense as much as anything. Certainly, the quarterback wants to conserve his time-outs whenever possible, and often he will use sideline passes hoping the receiver can get out of bounds after a catch. But the defense will try to prevent this by using a lot of zones, giving a few yards at a time. I will always take what the defense is giving because they cannot cover everywhere at once. Many times we have swept down the field, six or seven yards at a time, and suddenly were in field-goal range or knocking on the end zone for a touchdown. I am never fussy about how I move a team in this situation, just as long as we can move without any mistakes.

Conserving time-outs is an art and something that requires some preset planning. The quarterback must be aware of the time on the clock and the down and distance, as well as his position on the field. And if he can get a win or a tie with a field goal, he must always think about saving one time-out to get his field-goal unit onto the field, or barring that, have a play that, successful or unsuccessful, can stop the clock.

My friend Joe Theismann underscored this in Super Bowl XVII. With no time-outs and just a few seconds to play at the end of the first half, he wanted to edge closer for a field goal, so he hit Charley Brown on a pass near the sidelines. Unfortunately, it was not close enough to the sidelines to allow Charley to get out of bounds, so the clock ran out before Washington could get its field-goal unit in place. Joe has said many times he should simply have ignored that open receiver and thrown the ball away to stop the clock. While it did not mean the difference in that game, there are times where it could.

Calling time-outs is a shared responsibility between coach and quarterback. A coach, with his team trailing, will often use time-outs before the final two minutes to prevent the offense from dawdling along and wasting the clock, meaning that the quarterback must operate without them and get maximum offense in minimum time.

We did that in Super Bowl XVI when, with San Francisco leading 26–14, we got the ball with a minute and fifty-eight seconds to play and with only one time-out remaining. That meant we needed two possessions to get a victory and we took our shot—riding six plays for a touchdown and then having an opportunity for an onside kick and another try when there still were sixteen seconds to play. Unfortunately, the 49ers covered the kick, and we never had another chance. But there are times when kicks do bounce right for the guy needing another chance.

In situations such as we have just discussed, teams have something special, a "gadget play" some coaches call it. Sometimes after getting the ball on a turnover and the opposition is down, they reach into the bag of tricks and haul out a "flea-flicker" pass or a special reverse of some kind, usually with a forward pass as the capper. Gadget plays can be fake punts, either runs or passes, or fake field goals. Who can ever forget the sight of Seattle's place-kicker, Efren Herrera, running for a touchdown several years ago after a fake field goal, or Chester Marcol of the Packers circling away from his kicking position in a game against the Bears, and catching the winning touchdown pass? The psychological effects of these plays often are as decisive as the results they bring, and while they may seem like great fun to the fans—like something just drawn up on the spot—to be successful, they must be preplanned. A team must know going into the game whether the opposition is susceptible to being burned by these plays. If the punt-return team pressures your kicker on every play, then it is foolish to try a fake punt. However, if that unit has a tendency to drop back as soon as the ball is snapped in order to set up a good return, then it is ripe to be burned.

I believe that the time to call the flea-flicker, or double-reverse pass, is when things are going good in a game. A trick play during a time when we are having trouble really doesn't do us much good, and more often than not, it blows up in our faces. Field position is important, preferably with a chance to get a touchdown or a completion that can help to set up a score; and running the flea-flicker on first down, particularly with specialized personnel, is best because the defense might not notice the lineup changes. All of this, of course, is preplanned so that the team will not nullify a once-a-game maneuver.

Still vivid is a victory against Miami on a rainy Sunday in 1977 when our only two touchdowns came on "gadget" plays. One was a seventeen-yard quarterback sneak on a third-and-goal situation, the other a flea-flicker pass to our tight end, Bob Trumpy, which became the winning points. Both were by-products of pregame film study. The quarterback sneak was strictly between Bob Johnson, our center, and myself. I had noticed that the Dolphins, in certain long-yardage situations, brought in some specialty people and often did not put anyone over the center's nose. So Bob and I worked our own audible without telling the other nine players, and that was triggered by a code word while I called signals. As soon as Bob heard it, he snapped the ball and we were the only Bengals to move. This so stunned the Dolphins that before they could react, we were halfway to the end zone, and I tumbled over the goal line after one of the Miami players made a desperate lunge.

The flea-flicker came with about three minutes to play and the Bengals trailing, 17–16. I handed the ball to halfback Archie Griffin, sweeping to the right, and he then gave it to a wide receiver, John McDaniel, coming back to the left, as I retreated about seven yards. When McDaniel was opposite me, he tossed the ball back to me for a pass. In the meantime, the Miami defense, chasing Griffin and McDaniel, allowed Trumpy to slip into the end zone unnoticed and he easily caught the TD pass.

Perhaps the best of all the plays to run—and often the most important—are those that the quarterback uses to run out the clock. Knowledge of the rules governing the clock is as important here as it is in the two-minute drill, only this time the quarterback is trying to use as much time as he can. There also is a shared responsibility here between the offensive backs and receivers and the quarterback, in that those players must always try to stay in bounds. Many time-killing plays are sweeps and other wide plays, with the objective of using time, and too often the back will get so caught up in trying to make yardage that he forgets the clock's importance and runs out of bounds. A quarterback can remind his backs on every play, if necessary, that they should do nothing to stop the clock.

Pace is very important. Every team has a rhythm, but here the players should consciously slow down their route to the huddle, and the quarterback should take his time in giving the play. I try to get the team to the line of scrimmage with about fifteen seconds on the clock, and let them sit there in a preset position, with their hands on their knees. Then as the clock goes inside ten seconds I bring them to the set position and call the cadence evenly and perhaps a bit slower than usual. I will not set the linemen too soon and allow them to sit there, or use the stutter cadence, or draw out the signals too long lest the linemen, in their anxiety to end the game, move before the ball is snapped. If that happens, there is a penalty, the clock is stopped and the lost yardage makes it harder to get a first down that will keep possession of the ball—and the clock.

Of course, a quarterback need not tarry if the clock has been officially stopped because it does not begin again until the ball is snapped. A crisp play gets everyone moving together and with the good surge needed against a desperate defense.

The quarterback, of course, must take extra care in getting the snap, and here it goes right back to the precise mechanics of bringing the ball in to belt level and then dealing it out with the hands and the eyes to make sure the back gets it cleanly and there is no fumble. I suppose no one ever will forget the astounding ending to a Giants-Eagles game in 1978 when, on the supposed final play of the game, New York fullback Larry Csonka fumbled the handoff from quarterback Joe Pisarcik, and the ball was picked up and run in for a winning touchdown by defensive back Herman Edwards of Philadelphia. Since then, every winning team's favorite play formation is to have two tight ends in tight against the tackles, two running backs sitting just behind the quarterback and a wide receiver behind them . . . just in case the famous Fumble TD Play ever should happen again. When we line up this way, it means the clock cannot be stopped and we are nailing down a victory.

185

Chapter 8
Special Drills to Become a Better Quarterback

GOOD quarterbacks are not always born. Many of them are self-made; they take what natural skills they possess and then develop them through a program of intensive and consistent work in and out of season. Here, we will discuss the physical means by which a quarterback can improve his skills. We will present a series of drills that can improve his throwing accuracy, a suggested regimen for conditioning and maintaining that conditioning, some ideas that may help him become comfortable before a game, and a plan that hopefully can help him avoid the midseason blahs which affect so many players.

Since the physical skills of most quarterbacks are centered on their ability to throw the football, every care must be taken to be precise in doing that, whether in the game, practice or just loosening up. I always have felt very strongly that a quarterback must have a purpose in mind whenever and wherever he is loosening up. First should be improving his accuracy, and this begins in the simple act of playing catch with another person because it will carry over onto the field when the ball is going to receivers. There is a belief that if a quarterback will throw the ball at a person's body in practice, then he will be happy in a game to throw anywhere around it. Always reject this notion and be specific when throwing the ball. If the person with whom the quarterback is playing catch wears a helmet, then pick out the face mask and aim for it with every throw, because the more refined the throw, the more accurate it will be as a habit. This emphasis on accuracy should underscore every drill that is involved with throwing the football.

Here are some drills that have worked for me:

Throw on the Run: At the high school and college football levels, the ability to throw on the run is particularly important, because sprint-out quarterbacks are the vogue, and there is a necessity for some of this at the pro level. We have touched on the technique of throwing at the receiver—not leading him—when throwing on the run, and one of the great drills to help perfect this technique is to find a partner, set yourselves ten yards apart, and run up and down throwing the ball to each other.

In so doing, concentrate on getting the shoulders open to the target and throw directly at it. Not only does this hone a throwing skill but it also is a good conditioning drill, particularly after practice when coaches insist that the players do specialized running drills or sprints.

In the "throw-on-the-run" drill two quarterbacks can run along parallel lines, ten yards apart (photo 8-1), and concentrate on throwing the ball with the shoulders open to the target (photos 8-2 through 8-5). They also can sharpen the skill of throwing directly at the receiver while running (photos 8-6, 8-7) and not leading him.

8-1

8-2

190

8-3

8-4

8-5

8-6

8-7

191

Touch Drill: This will pay dividends at the times when a quarterback must scramble and still try to complete a pass over the linebackers and in front of the defensive backs. Start on a line ten yards in front of the goalposts, and station someone behind them to catch the ball as the passer runs from the right and from the left and lofts the ball over the goalpost crossbar. This forces him to get the ball up and drop it over something. Remember, it is a very rare person in football, especially linebackers, who can leap ten feet to knock away a pass.

We developed this drill after the 1981 season because we run plays putting me outside the linemen with no blockers as the tight end tries to sneak in behind the linebackers, and many times I must throw over the linebackers while running to my left. This means throwing across my body but I honed that skill with the touch drill, and the result is that we can run this kind of play both to the right and to the left and make the defense play us honest.

The "touch drill" improves the quarterback's ability to drop the ball between linebackers and defensive backs when he is on the move. He starts on a line ten yards in front of the goalposts (photos 8-8, 8-9) and, when he reaches the center support post, turns with his shoulders squared and tosses the ball over the crossbar (photos 8-10 through 8-13). This is successful only if the ball skims over the bar and into the arms of someone standing behind the goalposts. It can be repeated from the opposite direction (photos 8-14 through 8-19) to perfect the action from either side.

8-8

8-9

193

8-10

8-11

8-12

194

8-13

8-14

8-15

8-16

195

8-17

8-18

8-19

Throw Off the Knee: Place the right knee on the ground and play catch with someone. In so doing, throw to the right, center and left, opening the shoulders to face the target with each throw. This not only helps condition the throwing technique but also is a good way to loosen up before practice.

An adjunct to this drill is to stand and repeat it, with the feet together. This gets the thrower used to rotating his body to face his target.

Throwing off the knee before practice is a good drill to loosen up and perfect the throwing technique by opening the shoulders to throw (photos 8-20 through 8-26). It can be done in succession, throwing to the right, straight ahead and to the left, and can be repeated several times.

8-20   8-21   8-22   8-23

8-24   8-25   8-26

197

Wave-and-Scramble Drill: This has done me more good than anything else because it has helped my movement within the pocket. I can use a coach or another player standing about ten yards in front of me while I drop back to pass. At any point during the drop he can clap his hands, and that is a signal that I must stop and throw the football quickly, yet still get off a good throw. If he does not put his hands up by the time that I finish my drop, then I will set and shuffle up in the pocket, simulating the pass rush going around me. When I get a hand wave, right or left, I must move my feet in the direction indicated, but still keep the ball in the proper throwing position. If he gives me a sweeping motion with his arm, right or left, I scramble out of the pocket and we both run along parallel lines. When he puts his hands up, I will throw him the ball.

The "wave-and-scramble drill," noted here with a diagram and pictures, will help a quarterback's movement within the pocket. Using another person as a director, the quarterback sets up to pass (photo 8-27) and then is directed by a wave of the hand to move either to the left (photo 8-28) or back to the right (8-29) and then forward (8-30), and the process then can be repeated back to the left. When the director wants the ball thrown, he raises his hand, and the quarterback must throw at that moment, regardless of which way he is moving.

8-27

8-28

8-29

8-30

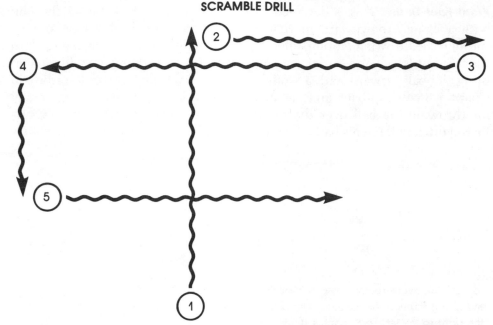

The diagram illustrates the course to be taken in the wave-and-scramble drill. No. 1 is the starting point for a drop-back move to point No. 2. The quarterback shuffles to his left to point No. 3 and then moves in the opposite direction to point No. 4. He then shuffles up a few steps, to simulate the pass rush moving around him, to point No. 5, where he begins his move to the left again to repeat the drill.

This drill helps a quarterback get used to moving in the pocket and conditions his mind because he must go through his pass patterns while being moved back and forth. It also is a great off-season leg conditioner.

There is another drill that the quarterback can use to check each of his pass plays, by tying it into the three-, five- or seven-step drop. Say, the play's progression goes from the flanker, to the tight end, to the fullback in the flat; so he will take a prescribed drop for that pattern, and as he hits his set point, his eyes focus immediately on the point where the flanker should be, and he opens his body to throw in that direction. Seeing that the flanker is not there, the quarterback shuffles up into the pocket and looks immediately to the spot where the tight end should be, and adjusts his body to be ready to throw at that spot. His final move will be to look for the fullback, move his body and then accurately throw the ball to someone simulating the fullback who has run that pass route.

The quarterback can do this for every one of his pass plays and the appropriate pass drop. Daily repetitions will condition his reflexes and decision-making, so that when he gets into a game, everything will be sharper and quicker.

Circle Drill: This involves three quarterbacks, who will run clockwise for a while, then counterclockwise. Each quarterback will throw to the man in front of him while on the run, getting used to throwing at different angles, as well as putting the ball where the receiver can catch it. Remember, it does not do any good to throw a nice, tight spiral on the run if it cannot be caught.

Front-Foot Drill: This is designed to help the quarterback throw the ball with a straight downward motion. He must raise up on his toes and go through the throwing motion, effecting the weight transfer from the right to the left foot (vice versa for left-handed throwers). In so doing, he will have to bring the ball forward with a straight overhand motion, as we described in Chapter 3 on drop-back and passing. This develops good habits, especially for throwing the ball over the middle, because a passer who throws flat-footed often will see his ball take off instead of go down toward the receiver.

The "front-foot drill" is designed to help the quarterback throw in a straight downward motion by raising up on his toes and going through the mechanics of throwing the ball as the weight is transferred from the right to the left foot (photos 8-31 through 8-34). It also helps him to gain some added height when throwing the ball.

8-31   8-32   8-33   8-34

This drill also helps the quarterback gain another advantage—he can become about two inches taller by raising up on his toes when throwing the ball. Consider the opposite: If the passer extends out too far with his feet planted solidly on the ground, he actually can lose inches from the natural top of his throwing arc, and that is when balls get batted down or, even worse, intercepted.

All of the foregoing drills, most of which are illustrated on these pages, will help the quarterback to hone his mechanics, mentally and physically. Now, how should he go about honing his body?

There is a big surge today in weight training, and many coaches, at all levels of competition, encourage their players to get into the weight rooms and pump as much iron as they can handle—often even more than they can handle. Only in the past few years have I become convinced that quarterbacks, who do not need the great upper body strength of other players, must do some weight work to keep muscles firm, to keep a good body tone and to help strengthen certain body parts, the shoulder joints, for instance. Even so, I will not work out on the real heavy weights, preferring the Nautilus machines we have at our practice facility, and in so doing I put particular emphasis on my legs, which are so importantly linked with throwing the ball. I use only light weights in toning my upper body, the objective being to maintain a full and easy range of motion that will not restrict my throwing.

I also will complete my throwing for the day before going to the weight lifting exercises, simply to avoid a possible fatigue factor, which could alter my throwing motion. That motion is something I almost jealously guard, and I will do anything possible to avoid the slightest hitch, lest I lose my groove and my accuracy suffers as a result.

In the off-season, I maintain my conditioning and flexibility with three days of weight work each week. I will run perhaps a mile and then do some sprints, but not until the cold weather has passed. I should stress that this program is my own personal preference, and all quarterbacks should consult their coaches and weight people before embarking on their own programs. Young athletes may not find the need for intense conditioning, but the older a player gets, the more he should get into a routine that will keep his weight down and his muscles firm.

Flexibility exercises are something else, and again an individual requirement. Our normal team routine, which consists primarily of stretching exercises done before every practice, satisfies most of my requirements during the season, to which I will add a couple of days of light weight lifting. However, there are some quarterbacks who require more stretching to loosen up, and if they cannot get it in the prepractice regimen, then they should do it on their own before practice begins, so they are ready to begin the practice routine as soon as exercises are complete.

During the week I will not go out early and throw to loosen up, because by the time we have finished our calisthenics and some of our prepractice routines, a half hour will have passed and I would have to loosen up all over again. A coach should be understanding and, if necessary, allow the quarterback time within the practice routine to get loose. I can accomplish some of this with the drills our receivers run to simulate keeping their feet in bounds after catching a short pass or working along the sidelines. We can throw the ball in an easy motion in these drills, and by the time we are called for the one-on-one or seven-on-seven work, our arms are ready to go all out.

Since I throw about a hundred balls in every practice session, I take care to keep my arm sound. In the early spring, once the weather gets warmer, I will start throwing either to work on some new things that we are going to put into our offense or as part of a conditioning program. And I never have had a tired arm when training camp begins.

Every quarterback knows when his arm begins to get tired, and he should knock off throwing to avoid a sore arm when that happens. I go strictly by feel, and if it becomes a labor to throw, I just quit for that day lest the fatigue start me developing bad habits.

Proper warm-up is the best way to avoid arm trouble. Couple that with a good throwing motion, and try to avoid anything that will strain an arm. That is not always possible, such as on a rainy practice day when the balls get heavy. Hardly realizing what is happening, the quarterback must throw the ball differently to compensate for the weight, and it will not be unusual for his arm to be a bit sore afterward.

There are plenty of road signs which should be read to avoid a sore arm. The bottom line is feeling comfortable after warming up, and our coaches always ask me whether I am ready to throw before beginning any heavy drills. If I need more time, I get it; if I am ready before they are, I will stop throwing and go on to something else. In a pregame situation, when I feel loose and comfortable with my throws, then my confidence level is where it should be. There are times in our pregame drills, particularly on cold days, when I want extra throwing because I just do not feel right, and I don't have the groove that I want. On hot days, I normally cut down my warm-up time to conserve energy.

A quarterback also can read his own throwing motion to notice any changes that could cause him problems. I can tell by my spiral, which comes from my straight overhand motion—something, by the way, that is much easier on the arm than a sidearm motion. My ball tends to go on a straight line, but if the nose starts to tail off, I know that my arm has dropped a bit. I simply concentrate on the straight overhand motion and forestall any potential arm problems.

Unlike baseball pitchers, who, if they suffer leg injuries, often alter their throwing motion and damage their arms, football quarterbacks seem more resilient in coping with hurts to their bodies. In 1981, I had the big toe on my right foot bent back during a regular-season game against the 49ers and could not finish the game. I had trouble planting my foot, and that affected my throwing motion, because I could not properly transfer my weight and thus I used more arm than normal. After the game, my arm was sore from the strain that change in delivery had caused. To compensate the next week—against the Steelers when we finally clinched our division title—I was outfitted with a special shoe to cushion that sore toe, and found that if I set up as comfortably as I could, transferred my weight quicker and threw with a bit more arm motion, I could do the job without any arm damage.

All of which shows that quarterbacks really are creatures of habit, and for many of us to be good, we must feel comfortable. That comfort is physical, mental and emotional, and while we are not high-strung performers such as opera and ballet stars, nonetheless there are routines and comforts that help to settle us into a good game-day groove.

My comfort zone begins during the practice week, because if I feel good then, I know I will feel good on Sunday. If the week is choppy, I will work as long as it takes in practice to get the comfortable feeling, because I am a player who plays like he practices. Finishing off the week feeling good eases my mind and gets me settled down. I know that if we have won a game and I did not feel that I prepared very well, I am dissatisfied, and I know the feeling long before the game is over, because throughout those sixty minutes, I never get comfortable. On the other hand, we have lost games but I prepared as well as I could, and I have come away, distraught that we lost, but satisfied that I could not have done anything more.

Like the off-season regimen we discussed earlier, being comfortable is an individual thing. What makes me feel comfortable may not appeal to someone else, so a quarterback—or any player, for that matter—should do what best appeals to him. Isaac Curtis, for instance, always cuts the arms off his T-shirts. A former linebacker, Jim LeClair, had equipment manager Tom Gray tape a protective pad over his right hand because Tom did it one year after Jim had hurt the hand and he went out and played a great game. When I get to the stadium, as I mentioned in outlining my own week's routine, I follow a regimen almost by the clock.

All of this can come under the heading of idiosyncrasies or superstitions, but really they are means to make a player feel comfortable and help him focus squarely on the game. I do it with my warm-ups, going out before the kickers and receivers—often when some of the coaches stroll out to visit their counterparts—and try to get loose so that when we get into our team pregame warm-ups I will be ready. If I feel comfortable before all of the team assembles for calisthenics, then I will just slow down my pace, and pick it back up when we go to the team warm-ups.

When we come back onto the field to begin the game, I go directly behind our bench and begin to loosen up again, particularly if we are to receive the kickoff. During the game, I also have routines, such as having someone waiting with a jacket on cold days, getting a glass of Gatorade and taking a gulp of water to wash away the drink's sweet taste before I go back onto the field. These do not seem like much, I know, but they all turn out to be that much less to think about during the game and help provide a tighter concentration on the game itself.

Quarterbacks at every level, it seems, always face a bit of a dip during the season. Young men playing in high school and college still are getting used to the routines and the pressures, and until their minds mature like their bodies, they feel the fatigue factor. In professional football, we do too, because a sixteen-game season, coupled with four in the preseason plus the training camp, does place a strain on mind and body. There is no predicting when a dip will come, and much of it is predicated on individual and team success. Certainly, in our Super Bowl drive in 1981, no one felt any fatigue or strain when we blew down one team after another for most of the season. It did catch up to us in the final month, but by that time we were on the brink of a division title, so we had some extra incentives to keep us going.

I do believe that a player's conditioning has much to do with surviving the blahs. A quarterback will be more consistent over the full season if he is in the best possible physical condition. If the team stays healthy, that has an effect because he will have the same people working with him all the time. Scheduling also is a factor. Two or three games in a row on the road can be tough; two or three at home are a pleasure because routines remain the same and the home crowd always is there to boost the team. Having to play on Monday and Thursday nights also makes a difference because the practice week is drastically changed, therefore so are the routines. Having tough teams on the schedule does not bother me because I enjoy the competition and our team seems to play better against these teams than against weaker ones, so it really does not seem to make any difference if we get two or three tough games in a row.

I believe that part of the key to alleviating the hills and valleys is a gradual buildup to every game. Playing once a week allows plenty of time to forget one game and get ready for the next, but where some players come apart is being ready emotionally to play on Saturday and the game still is to be played on Sunday. This is one of the techniques of coaching, knowing when and how to have a team primed for one o'clock on Sunday afternoon.

Paul Brown was a master of doing this. He did not immerse himself in the technicalities of the game plan, though he certainly knew and approved of all that we would do in a game. But he was meticulous in the way that he prepared us mentally, talking to us every day, making the decisions on how everything that we did was organized, and seeing that every player was exactly where he should be in our overall plan. There was the feeling of being on a train that hit every station exactly on time, and somehow when the journey ended, that train would come to a very smooth stop.

That certitude was passed on to the players, particularly to the quarterbacks, and it helped them in their preparation. I know one thing for sure—it helped me, and all that I learned during that time has stayed with me to this day. For which I am very thankful.

Chapter 9
The Streak

EVERYTHING we have discussed sounds so good and appears so attainable, but the real test of how a quarterback can be rated comes in a game. That is the final exam for all of the homework that he does, all of the practice time and consultation, where all of his experience and know-how come into play and really are put on the line on a put-up or shut-up basis.

I have cited many games where successful plays worked for us, but among the hundreds of games I have played on every level, the most satisfying has to be our final game of the 1982 season against the Houston Oilers when I established an all-time National Football League record of twenty straight pass completions, which in turn led to a season completion record and the NFL passing title for a second straight year.

Earlier in the book I cited the "hot-hand" syndrome, and nowhere was this better evidenced than in the game against the Oilers when, beginning in the first quarter and lasting until late in the third quarter, I did not miss a receiver. Sure, there was a bit of luck when one pass fell incomplete but we got a reprieve when Houston had a dual penalty of offsides and pass interference, but as in any situation where a player or a team is on a hot roll, there must be some good fortune involved.

My good fortune came in the form of that penalty and the work which my receivers did to get open, and they made a couple of very difficult catches which just as easily could have missed the mark. This also was a perfect example of a quarterback being able to read so clearly what the defense was doing, and working in close mental harmony with the receivers, who had to be reading the same thing as they ran their routes.

I certainly am not a greedy quarterback and I never have placed my own personal records above team success, but I take particular pride in this accomplishment because I believe it epitomizes the best any passer can do under the combat conditions of a game. Why, I have wondered, was I able to do it against one team on a certain day and not do it several times a season against other teams? I cannot answer that question and neither can anyone else, except to say that it really was "one of those days," and so much so that had it not been for a dropped swing pass by Pete Johnson on the play before the streak began, the record easily could have been twenty-four straight completions.

The first time that we had the ball, I completed all three of my throws in a 35-yard scoring drive, the last of one yard to Danny Ross. When we got the ball a second time, our second play was a pass to Pete, which he simply did not handle, and I must say it is one of the few times that this fine fullback ever muffed one of those throws. It can happen to anyone, and at the time, it was insignificant as far as any records were concerned, because no one ever could imagine that I would reel off such a string of completions.

The Oilers are a team that we face twice a year, so their personnel and defensive style are well known to us. In this game they did not do anything radically different from previous times, playing a standard zone defense, with three linemen up front and four linebackers. It then became a matter of execution on our part, and everyone did his share. Our linemen were great in providing protection; in reviewing the films, I did not see one instance where I was particularly harried so that I had to throw quickly, which certainly is one way to bust up any kind of streak. We interspersed our running with the passing, and this further kept the Oilers' defense a bit off balance because it could not key on our passing game.

After Johnson missed that pass, the streak began quite innocently enough with a quick toss to Steve Kreider, and with a deft move, he turned what might have been a 5-yard gain into a 25-yard gain that moved the ball from Cincinnati's 31-yard line to the Oilers' 44-yard line. I threw only one other pass in this drive, a 9-yard shot to Cris Collinsworth that put the ball at Houston's 10-yard line, where Archie Griffin then swept right end for the score on the next play.

Here is how the rest of that record-setting sequence followed:

(Cincinnati led, 14–10, early in the second quarter when we got the ball for the third time in the game.)

First-and-ten, Bengals' 23-yard line: Checking my progression list and finding Ross and Collinsworth covered, I went to Pete Johnson circling out of the backfield, and he caught a pass for 14 yards, to our 37-yard line.

First-and-ten, Bengals' 37-yard line: Collinsworth caught a ball along the right sideline for a gain of 13 yards. This play set up a great touchdown pass completion later in the second half to Isaac Curtis and, to my mind, was one of the most important receptions made during the streak.

First-and-ten, midfield: Danny Ross, from the left, came open after reading the Oilers' coverage, and he turned an 8-yard catch into an 18-yard gain, to Houston's 32-yard line.

First-and-ten, Oilers' 28-yard line: After Pete Johnson had gained 4 yards, Ross lined up on the right and circled in front of linebacker Greg Bingham and caught a pass to gain 15 yards, to the Oilers' 13-yard line.

Two plays later, I was sacked, fumbled and lost the ball at Houston's 20-yard line, where it was picked up and returned 50 yards by defensive end Jesse Baker. The streak at this point was six-for-six.

Houston had pulled to within a point at 14–13 following that fumble recovery, and we began our next series at our 20-yard line.

First-and-ten, Bengals' 20-yard line: Charles Alexander swung out of the backfield, and as the first receiver on my progression list, he gained 14 yards to the 34-yard line.

First-and-ten, Bengals' 34-yard line: Collinsworth lined up on the left, and curled to the outside where I hit him with a 6-yard pass.

First-and-ten, Bengals' 49-yard line: After two runs, we put in two tight ends, M. L. Harris and Ross, and I found Harris over the middle for a 15-yard gain.

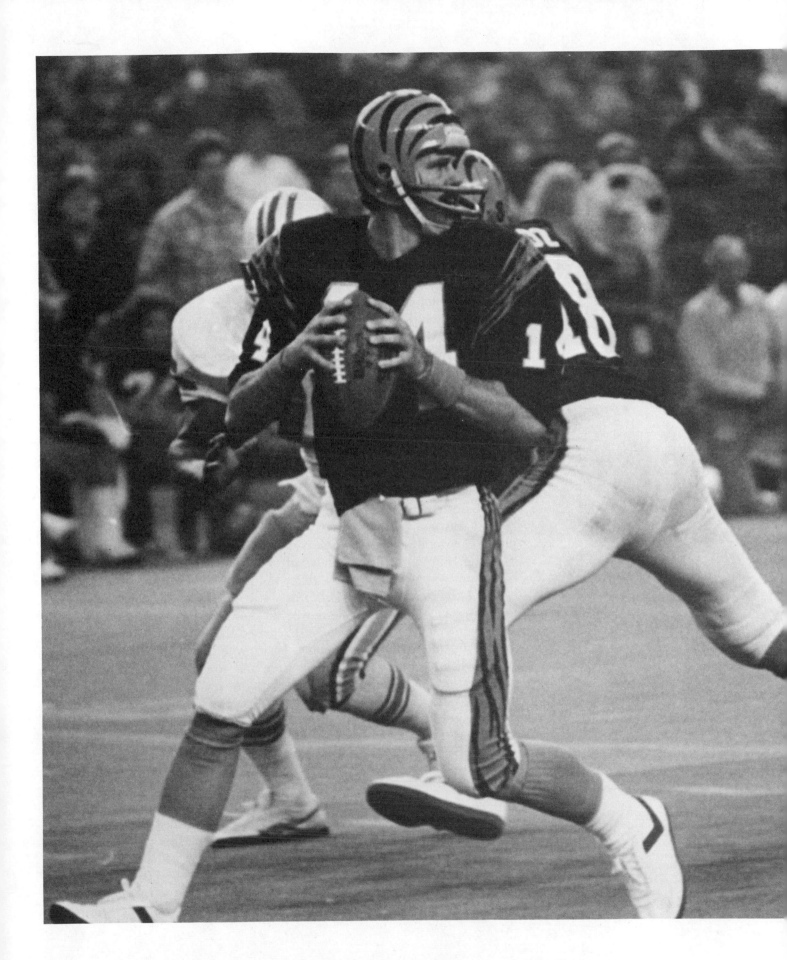

Second-and-nine, Oilers' 35-yard line: After Alexander gained a yard rushing, we set up with three wide receivers plus Ross at tight end. Dan worked himself loose in the middle again—simply a read on the defense that moved him into a seam—and he gained 13 yards.

First-and-ten, Oilers' 22-yard line: Houston was giving us the middle, and Ross went back in and picked up 8 more yards.

Third-and-eleven, Oilers' 23-yard line: After Johnson's run, and an apparent 13-yard TD run by Alexander was nullified by a holding penalty, I missed on a pass to Kreider, but it wasn't Steve's fault because he was pushed by Carter Hartwig, who was the nickel back, and the officials spotted the foul. We got a first down and the incompletion was expunged by the penalty.

Second-and-six, Oilers' 12-yard line: Alexander again swung out of the backfield as my primary receiver close to the goal line, gaining 4 yards.

Third-and-two, Oilers' 8-yard line: Isaac Curtis ran an outside pattern, against man-for-man coverage, and I quickly found him for a 7-yard gain, to the 1-yard line. Johnson swept right for the score on the next play and we led, 21–13, with two minutes to play in the half. We did not get the ball again that quarter for any passes, as I killed the clock by falling on the ball in the last 14 seconds.

At the half-time break, I found out later, some of the players knew that I had completed thirteen straight passes, but no one said anything to me. Dave Lapham told me later it was like the pitcher who has a no-hitter going into the seventh inning. "No one wants to mention it and break the spell," Dave said, "and we figured we didn't want to break your spell, either." I'm sure most pitchers are aware they have no-hitters going because they can see the scoreboards where runs and hits are posted, but in a football game, consecutive passes completed are not something visible to everyone, and while I knew I was in a good groove, I was so engrossed in the game and trying to pull away from those pesky Oilers that I had no idea of any such streak.

When Houston could not move after the second-half kickoff, we got the ball at our 48-yard line, and we twice ran Pete Johnson for a gain of 8 yards.

Third-and-two, Oilers' 44-yard line: Issac Curtis lined up on the right and took off, giving a quick inside move and then streaked for the goal line. He was my man all the way, and after I released the ball, I thought it was going to be a bit too long. But somehow, Isaac, who had made some astounding catches before, outdid himself this time and stretched his right arm to its fullest extension and grasped the ball with one hand as it came down, never breaking stride as a defender, Willie Tullis, was with him almost step-for-step. He just kept going into the end zone for the touchdown. As I noted, an earlier pass to Collinsworth helped to set this up because the pattern was the same, and the Oilers moved immediately to cover Collinsworth, allowing Isaac to break free and get a step on Tullis. This is a perfect example of how a quarterback can use his receivers to set up patterns.

When we got the ball again, Archie Griffin gained four yards on a trap play, and on second-and-six, at the Bengals' 33, Alexander circled out of the backfield and caught a five-yard pass. We missed the first down on the next play and punted.

Houston couldn't move and punted back, where we got the ball, *first-and-ten, Bengals' 31-yard line:* Dan Ross once more lined up to the right, saw his coverage and moved over to catch a 12-yard pass. I know this sounds monotonously easy, but Dan was simply doing his job and coming open quickly so I did not have to look around for someone to get the ball. His actions are determined by what the defense does, and simply stated, if its coverage is to the right, he will go to the left, and if the coverage is to his left, he will move to his right. Both of us must read this together, and that day against Houston, our reads were perfect.

First-and-ten, Bengals' 43-yard line: Collinsworth ran a quick-out pattern to the left and gained four yards. On the following play, we were penalized for an illegal block after a one-yard gain by David Verser's end around.

Second-and-15, Bengals' 38-yard line: We put three wide receivers into the game and Kreider ran a quick turn out to the left for a gain of four yards, to the 42-yard line. That pass completion tied the record of eighteen straight completions which Steve DeBerg of the Denver Broncos had just established the previous week. Steve did his over two games, getting seventeen in a row against the Rams, and then hitting his first the following game against the Kansas City Chiefs. Until then, the record had been seventeen straight by Bert Jones, in 1974, when he played for the Baltimore Colts.

There was no announcement of that fact in the stadium, so I naturally still was oblivious to all of the record-setting. I am sure the Oilers' public relations people deliberately withheld the information from the crowd with the same mind-set that Dave Lapham used in equating not telling a pitcher that he has a no-hitter in progress. I never will know what my reactions would have been had an announcement been made, but in reflection, I am pleased that nothing was said, because it meant my concentration on the game remained intact.

Third-and-eleven, Bengals' 42-yard line: Again, we had three wide receivers in the game, with Verser lined up on the right. He went down the field and ran a great pattern into a lot of traffic to make a very difficult catch that not only set the record but also gained 17 yards. David was my main man all the way on that play, and I really pushed the ball into some tight coverage to get to him, but he made it look a lot easier with his move to get open and then catching the ball a bit off balance. Houston was in its nickel defense at the time, and with three wide outs and a tight end in the pattern, we forced them to cover a lot of territory. I'm sure they felt I would go to Collinsworth in that situation, but I really did not look for Cris because I felt that David would get open for a bigger gain, and he did.

Second-and-ten, Oilers' 41-yard line: Danny Ross did his usual read and came free to catch a nine-yard pass, the twentieth in a row. Still no announcement to the crowd, but by now, the press box knew of the record and had begun its own tabulation. I never did know whether our bench was aware of the record because our play-calling went along as if nothing unusual was afoot. We called two more runs, the last of which was called back because of a holding penalty, so we were faced with long yardage for another first-down play.

First-and-eighteen, Oilers' 37-yard line: Dan Ross got free in the middle, but this time, I simply underthrew the ball, bouncing it to him on two hops. The streak had ended, but I really ended it myself with a poor throw, for which I am glad because I would not have wanted someone to drop a ball or make a mistake that might have caused some regret.

At this point, there were about four minutes to play in the third quarter.

The streak had begun at about the four-minute mark of the first quarter, so for a half game I had been perfect. When I checked back on all that had happened during that time, I was happy to note that this record didn't come about simply by dumping the ball to a back all the time. Rather, eight different receivers caught passes—four wide receivers, two tight ends and two backs. Eleven of the twenty catches were for more than twelve yards, and the record-breaker was a seventeen-yarder, which certainly is no chippie. Perhaps that is the pass I'm most proud of—not taking anything away from Isaac Curtis' great touchdown catch—because I completed a tough pass to get that record.

That performance also helped me to establish a single-season completion mark of 70.55 percent and that broke a 37-season mark that Sammy Baugh, a great quarterback for the Washington Redskins who is in the Hall of Fame, had set back in 1945. His mark was 70.33, during a ten-game season in which he completed 128 of 182 passes. My mark came in a nine-game season (abbreviated because of the players' strike) but I threw 309 passes and completed 218. To tell the truth, I was not even aware that Sammy had such a record or even what the record for completions in a single season really was until someone mentioned it during the postgame interviews. But I still was so stunned at the streak that it really didn't rub off on me too much.

Of course, my friend Collinsworth couldn't resist one of his good-natured barbs at my age, wondering to the press whether Sammy would be happy for me "because they were teammates." Cris thinks anyone over thirty played in the single-wing era, though Sammy Baugh had made the transition to T-formation quarterback at the time, and his record had helped the Redskins into the NFL championship game in 1945.

I guess when I judge both records, the accuracy mark of Baugh's means the most because every quarterback prides himself on getting the ball to his receivers, and if that happens, then the important mark of consistency will follow. Accuracy and consistency go hand-in-hand, and that is really what we have discussed in touching all of the areas that a quarterback must cover to be successful.

If there is one other statistical record that I would like to own when I retire, I guess it would be the career completion mark. Then I will have done my job to the best of my ability, and anyone can be proud of that accolade. That, of course, remains for the future and will take a backseat to my own team-oriented goals of getting another shot or two at a Super Bowl title. That is the true art of quarterbacking.

Index

217

ABOUT THE AUTHORS

Cincinnati Bengals quarterback Ken Anderson has accumulated more than 30,000 yards from passing during his NFL career, placing him among the top ten in this category, and has been named to the Pro Bowl team several times. He has ranked No. 1 among all NFL passers four times (1974, 1975, 1981 and 1982) during his career. A collegiate performer at little-known Augustana College, Rock Island, Illinois, he was signed as the Bengals' third-round draft choice in 1971 and won an NFL starting position by the end of his rookie season.

Jack Clary is a free-lance author with more than a dozen books on sports to his credit. They include *Careers in Sports, Pro Football's Great Moments, The Gamemakers* and coauthorship with Paul Brown of that famed coach's autobiography, *PB*. Clary, head of Sports Media Enterprises, a consulting firm in Stow, Mass., also worked for seventeen years as a daily journalist and columnist for The Associated Press, New York *World Telegram & Sun* and the Boston *Herald Traveler*, and is a regular contributor to *PRO!* magazine.